ADVANCE PRAISE FOR
When Did Everybody Else Get So Old?

"Delightful and poignant . . . a book to cherish and to share with those you love."

—**Dale Hanson Bourke**, author of *Embracing Your Second Calling*

"Jennifer Grant is fiercely tender, funny, passionate about family, faithful, and hungry for justice. Read this book!"

—**Becca Stevens**, founder of Thistle Farms and a top ten 2016 CNN Hero

"A simply magnificent meditation on middle age . . . an obvious labor of love and joy that appears like a friend at your side and starts walking with you, doling out stories that will make you roar with laughter, bring tears to your eyes, impart practical wisdom, and make you absolutely sure that you are not alone in this."

—**Cathleen Falsani**, journalist and author of *The God Factor*

"This beautiful book belongs on every woman's nightstand (probably alongside her favorite jar of wrinkle cream)."

—**Katherine Willis Pershey**, author of *Very Married*

"Jennifer Grant's shimmering prose, soulful observations, wit, and insight make her an apt companion as we move through this necessary life stage of change and growth."

—**Michelle Van Loon**, author of *Moments and Days*

"Jennifer Grant manages to convey the trials of midlife with both realism and hope. This memoir, unexpectedly, helped me look forward to experiencing my forties and fifties."

—**Dorcas Cheng-Tozun**, author of *Start, Love, Repeat*

"It's rare to read someone who is as honest as Jennifer Grant is. In a time that's full to overflowing with easy, posturing confessions, this is a necessary, awakening memoir."
—**Jon M. Sweeney**, coauthor of *Mixed-Up Love* and editor of *Phyllis Tickle: Essential Spiritual Writings*

"I didn't know how much I needed this book until I read it. It gave me much-needed language for midlife's bruising and beautiful change. Grant's memoir is tender and funny in all the right places, and I can't wait to recommend it to friends!"
—**Jen Pollock Michel**, author of *Teach Us to Want* and *Keeping Place*

"The perfect companion to walk with on this road through the unexpected joy and grief of middle age."
—**Carla Barnhill**, author of *The Myth of the Perfect Mother*

"Readers will find a true friend in Jennifer Grant's beautifully crafted memoir of her forties. Highly recommended!"
—**Keri Wyatt Kent**, author of *Deeply Loved* and *Godspace*

"A brilliant memoir about the harshness and freedom of midlife. Bonus: A writer who can work Richard Rohr, Martha Stewart, and David Sedaris into one book must be read."
—**Lesa Engelthaler**, writer and nonprofit executive recruiter

"Hilarious and heartbreaking . . . a must-read for anyone who seeks to savor this amazing season of life."
—**Caryn Rivadeneira**, author of *Broke*

WHEN DID EVERYBODY ELSE GET SO OLD?

INDIGNITIES, COMPROMISES, AND THE UNEXPECTED GRACE OF MIDLIFE

WHEN DID EVERYBODY ELSE GET SO OLD?

INDIGNITIES, COMPROMISES, AND THE UNEXPECTED GRACE OF MIDLIFE

Jennifer Grant

Herald Press

Harrisonburg, Virginia

Library of Congress Cataloging-in-Publication Data
Names: Grant, Jennifer, author.
Title: When did everybody else get so old? : indignities, compromises, and
 the unexpected grace of midlife / Jennifer Grant.
Description: Harrisonburg : Herald Press, 2017. | Includes bibliographical
 references.
Identifiers: LCCN 2016052580| ISBN 9781513801315 (pbk. : alk. paper) | ISBN
 9781513801384 (hardcover : alk. paper)
Subjects: LCSH: Older Christians--Religious life. | Aging--Religious
 aspects--Christianity. | Middle-aged persons--Religious life.
Classification: LCC BV4580 .G7265 2017 | DDC 248.8/5--dc23 LC record
available at https://lccn.loc.gov/2016052580

Unless otherwise indicated, all Scripture quotations are taken from the Holy
Bible, New Living Translation, copyright © 1996, 2004, 2007 by Tyndale
House Foundation. Used by permission of Tyndale House Publishers, Inc.,
Carol Stream, Illinois 60188. All rights reserved.

Chapter 9 is adapted from "Of Teenagers and Flight Attendants," *Aleteia/
FOR HER*, January 26, 2016. Read it in its entirety at http://forher.aleteia
.org/articles/of-teenagers-flight-attendants/. Chapter 17 contains lines from
the essay "In Praise of the Tenacity of Marriage," *Aleteia/FOR HER*, published on January 26, 2016. Read it at http://forher.aleteia.org/articles/
in-praise-of-the-tenacity-of-marriage/.

WHEN DID EVERYBODY ELSE GET SO OLD?
© 2017 by Jennifer Grant.
Released by Herald Press, Harrisonburg, Virginia 22802. 800-245-7894.
All rights reserved.
Library of Congress Control Number: 2016052580
International Standard Book Number: 978-1-5138-0131-5 (paper);
 978-1-5138-0138-4 (hardcover); 978-1-5138-0132-2 (ebook)
Printed in United States of America
Design by Merrill Miller
Cover design incorporates mulitple images including a photo by
 MarkUK97 / iStockphoto / Thinkstock.
Author photo by Ian Grant-Funck

21 20 19 18 17   10 9 8 7 6 5 4 3 2 1

For Keiko

Do not regret growing older—
it is a privilege denied to many.

Unknown

CONTENTS

Foreword

*W*hat *is* middle age, anyway? Fortyish? But suppose I die at forty-two? Was I middle-aged at twenty-one?

Do the math along with Jennifer Grant in *When Did Everybody Else Get So Old?* With her, you will see it is impossible to understand middle age by multiplying and dividing. We need something more finely calibrated, more accurate.

Centuries ago, we began to invent the concept of "childhood." Now we need to hone definitions of stages in our adult lives. As many of us live to be older, as the oldest of us enjoy twenty-twenty eyesight thanks to cataract operations, as we stay mobile by exercising at the gym, as we watch our grandchildren raise their children, adulthood lengthens and challenges us to define its recognizable way stations. "Middle age" is among the most provocative and confusing of all the adult phases. What is it? What does it mean?

In this book, Jennifer Grant offers a significant contribution to our understanding of middle age. As she suggests in nineteen brief, funny, confessional chapters, midlife does not arrive at the same age for everyone. You recognize your own midlife when your children begin walking ahead of you on the sidewalk because they don't want to be seen with you. When you develop aches and pains in joints you never knew you had. When you begin to watch your parents age. When it starts to seem plausible that you might sometime actually die.

After that realization, you might live more intentionally. You work at unearthing memories of your own past, and you act with an eye to your future. You begin to imagine yourself looking back on the choices you are now making and assessing those choices, and therefore you make choices more intentionally. If you are patient and reflective, you might even grasp your life as a sweep of time, your life as a whole. Your childhood and your old age join hands. Your middle-aged self becomes friends with those other parts of yourself.

In this book, we watch Jennifer Grant going about that work. Here she is, emerging from the drudgery and physical work of changing diapers and filling sippy cups to the shock of recognition that she is suddenly in midlife. In her new retro glasses, which her daughter informs her are not chic, this woman who is "a little lost, a little lumpy," as she puts it, becomes a disarming model for us. She undergoes the rite of passage that is middle age right in front of our very eyes—navigating the loss of her children, one by one, to college; freaking out over her deficient resume; steering through the rapids of marriage; experiencing friends fall away when her children no longer play baseball with local teams. She takes us with her to her last tea with a dear, terminally ill friend. We suffer with her as she discovers she cannot protect her beloved sister from either her depression or her cancer.

We also follow Grant as she recovers from the failures of her body and her grief over her sister's death. She looks back, examines what has happened. She begins to gather her life into a story line. It is always harder to make a reader believe in hope than in despair. And yet in these chapters, Grant performs some of the magic of recovery. She is surprised by unexpected words, by her kids' jokes, by the tallness of her son, by the healing power of waking up to another new day. Simple magic; magic we can follow. She ages. She changes. She is scrupulously fair, often hilarious, sometimes wounded and angry. But she is capable of looking up and seeing that the weather will change.

I admire the way Grant describes middle age as both disappointment and joy. It is a place where the ridiculous and the sublime mix. Last winter's clothes no longer fit her, but her husband and her adolescent children do harmonize, at least sometimes. Grant's book zings briskly between the "hunks and colors" of this earth, as Richard Wilbur put it, and a transcendent sense of what those hunks and colors signify. The ridiculous and the sublime have equal weight in this book because, in midlife, they rub up against one another with such friction.

I am grateful to have read this book. I wish you happiness as you accompany Jennifer Grant on her journey through middle age.

—Jeanne Murray Walker,
author of *The Geography of Memory*

Memory, Seahorses, and Telling It Slant

I'm standing at the end of the driveway, hot asphalt stinging the soles of my feet. Somewhere out of sight, an ice cream truck trills out "The Entertainer." The boys across the street call out my brother's name, and he sprints over to them, brandishing a stick and a metal trashcan lid. Flying by overhead, an airplane leaves a white streak across the face of the sky, and the cicadas sing their endless, grating song.

I don't know why these images and not others come to mind when I remember being a child in late summer in the Chicago suburbs. We don't choose which moments cut themselves into our memories, like lovers' initials hacked into tree trunks or dirty words scraped into the thin paint of a bathroom stall. C. S. Lewis described his memory as haphazard and selective;[1] yours and mine are too. And how and why we remember what we do is a stunning mystery—down to the places in the body where memories are stored.

Near the center of the brain is the hippocampus, named for its bizarre resemblance to a seahorse. Picture a long, curved tail proceeding from a broad, upper structure and snout. This part of the limbic system—where emotion, motivation, and even the sense of smell are housed—is responsible for long-term memory storage. People with Alzheimer's disease, some seizure disorders, and schizophrenia have been found to have atrophied hippocampi. Sometimes they can't find their way around in familiar places or remember the names or faces of people they've loved for a lifetime. It's a terrifying prospect, losing the ability to remember, and most of us fear Alzheimer's more than cancer.

But where do our memories go when we forget?

Where do they go when we die?

After transplant surgery, some organ recipients insist that the memories of their donors were sewn into their bodies along with a new heart or kidney. They claim to "remember" the preferences, names, and even circumstances of death of those from whom the organs were harvested. A person with a new lung suddenly has a taste for beer or classical music. A child with a new liver has nightmares that echo the tragic death of her donor.

Most of us have complicated relationships with our memories; some of them bring comfort, but others disturb and haunt us. Good or bad, memories are always works in progress—changeable, evolving, imperfect. Although Emily Dickinson cautioned that we "tell all the truth, but tell it slant,"[2] those of us who write personal essays and memoir seldom need the tip. No matter how rigorous we are, our remembering is always skewed . . . even if we track down our classmates after forty years to confirm that our second-grade teacher *really* wore those orange bell-bottoms, or if we pour over old photographs to pinpoint the year when we traded childhood's ease for self-consciousness.

We write as honestly as we can about our flaws and fantasies, but our hardworking, insatiable egos ensure that the remembering of our lives is always slant.

"The heart's memory eliminates the bad and magnifies the good," wrote novelist Gabriel García Márquez.[3] He said that purging bad memories makes us more able to bear the burdens of the past. It doesn't help that the ego is an indulgent cinematographer, creating a biopic in which we're cast as sympathetic protagonists, framed in the softest, most flattering light. Thanks to my ego, I default to seeing myself as reasonable and well-intentioned—and certainly more wronged than ever wrong myself. The employer who failed to promote me, the friend who proved false, the stranger who flipped me off in the parking garage: they all morph into smirking, disfigured caricatures when I think back on them. I imagine you do the same thing.

In their book, *Mistakes Were Made (but Not by Me)*, social psychologists Carol Tavris and Elliot Aronson explore memory, self-justification, and how we construct the often flawed and egocentric stories of our lives. They describe the process by which we make sense of our experiences as like that of assembling shards of glass or pieces of broken pottery into a mosaic.

> From the distance of years, we see the mosaic's pattern. It seems tangible, unchangeable; we can't imagine how we could reconfigure those pieces into another design. But it is a result of years of telling our story, shaping it into a life narrative that is complete with heroes and villains, an account of how we came to be the way we are.[4]

Constructing that narrative "mosaic" out of the rubble of what we've managed to remember (or could not possibly forget) can also can fool us into believing that we can be summed up by what has happened to us or by what we've achieved in our lives. We begin to believe that our biography *is* our identity. We forget that who we really are—that interplay between our bodies, minds, and spirits—is a beautiful mystery and not simply the sum total of our life events.

But this framing and reframing of our own memories isn't all bad. It can help us recognize how we've grown, nudge us toward letting go of regret, and leave us feeling freshly grateful for loving friends and other gifts that we are prone to overlook. But we also trick ourselves. Tavris and Aronson admit that even they—experts on the subject of self-justification—can be blind to their own biases and self-deceit. Just like all of us. *This is who I am. This is how I got here. That teacher made all the difference. This loss changed me. That moment was pure magic. Here's what I was missing. Here's why my life matters.*

Richard Rohr writes that the concocted self is who we think we are, but our true self is who we have always been—it's our eternal essence, or soul—and that it's in the second half of our lives when we rediscover these true selves.[5] It's been in my forties that I've started to break free of the notion that what I remember or what's gone very right or very wrong in my life is *who I am.*

In this decade when false affections fade away, disappointments mount, and life gets real, I've begun to grasp that I am *not*—for better or for worse—that patchwork quilt of a biography that I've been writing and editing and uploading to my long-term memory all my life. It's as though I'm going through a thaw. Bit by jagged bit, an icy shellac falls away. Without its protective coating, my faults come into clearer view, and I must accept my own biases and limitations. I'm warier about my own emotions, no longer looking to them as dependable guides. There are loose ends in my life that won't be tied up neatly, shattered relationships I can't repair, and puzzles whose missing pieces will remain lost.

I started my forties looking too often into the mirror and getting tangled up in my thoughts—my goals, my shifting identity, my disappointments, my hopes. As I leave this decade behind, I find myself focusing less on me and more on how I might, bit by incremental bit, make the world more whole. That old, invented self with her fragile ego seems like an acquaintance with whom I've lost touch. I remember what her face looks like, but I can't quite remember the sound of her voice. There's a freedom that accompanies letting go of the concocted self. I'm more ready to stand back and observe a situation from a distance. I hold my memories more loosely, even the ones that have cast the longest shadows over my life. I see the wisdom of the writer of Ecclesiastes who directs me to enjoy what I actually have instead of chasing after what isn't mine (Ecclesiastes 6:9).

I recently texted my friend Caryn, a friend with whom I dip into and then pop out of deep discussions on the phone while she and I are twenty miles away from each other, sitting in our parked cars waiting to pick up our kids after school or standing in line at the grocery store.

"More and more, I'm falling in love with Ecclesiastes," I wrote. "To everything there is a season."

"I love that book," she responded, ever game to receive one of my random texts and grab hold of the conversation. "Weary, wise, contradictory. And yet somehow happy."

"Exactly," I answered. "It's about resignation, surrender even, but also about finding joy. About trust, really. Trusting that all will be well, even when nothing is making sense."

"Yeah," she texted back. "Waving that flag of surrender. Knowing it's all going to be okay."

My daughter Isabel and I recently spent a few days together in Scotland. In the Highland town of Nethy Bridge, we took a two-hour, guided walk through the pine forest in the Cairngorms National Park. We were a small group: my daughter and me, a Scot named Iver who appeared to be in his late fifties, and our guide. Iver came very prepared for the outing with binoculars, rain gear, and what seemed like a hundred questions about regional wildlife. Our ranger, Allison, delighted in teaching us about the ecosystem. She introduced new species to us, including the western capercaillie, a frighteningly large grouse that looks like a cross between a crow and a turkey. She boasted about the ground cover, called blaeberry, telling us that because it is healthy, the whole forest flourishes. She persuaded us to taste the wild chanterelle mushrooms that grow alongside the path—only by assuring us that they aren't poisonous by tearing off a corner and nibbling first.

After a rich afternoon, one particular moment remains with me. Allison pointed out a section of young pines and noted that they looked crammed together, growing in a clump, almost haphazardly. She then showed us a patch of mature pines. The trees stood a neat distance from each other, tall and straight, allowing the sun to shine in between them onto the blaeberry.

"It takes a while," Allison said. "But by the time it's about forty or fifty years old, the forest has sorted itself out."

Mary Karr has said it takes a lifetime of struggle to get used to who you are.[6] I agree, but hope that maybe—like someone practicing the piano for years or making risotto for the sixth time—I'm beginning to see progress. This book is a memoir of my forties. All the stories in this book are true, in the way our memories are, but I have altered some names and details to respect the privacy of others. Passages about my children are, perhaps, the most "slant." Over the years, I've been more cautious about what I write about them, so you'll understand why I don't always use their proper names and that I sometimes reflect in a broader way about what it's like to be a mother of adolescents than to tell very personal anecdotes about them. (Oh, the stories I could tell . . . if I wanted to be sure they'd never speak to me again.) These stories follow one another in a loosely chronological way. Early chapters in the book describe my sometimes turbulent approach and landing into my forties; the events in later chapters happened more recently, on the brink of fifty.

I regard midlife as the beginning of life's compelling third act—not just as a time of chin hairs and disappointment. In middle age, like the mature pines in the Cairngorms, we've gotten ourselves more sorted out. Our roots deeper and trunks stronger than when we were young, we can stand tall, poised to help the rest of the forest thrive.

ONE

Yahweh, Meet Me Halfway

The city of Detroit holds a strange charm for me. It was home to my mother's parents, and although they died decades before I was born, they have captured my imagination ever since I was a child. I don't know much about them. She was a flapper and quite beautiful; he a poet and bootlegger on the wrong side of the law. They fled across the bridge to Canada, where, later, my mother was born.

Their lives must have been very hard; my grandmother died of tuberculosis when she was just past thirty. But my romantic imagination about them—and of Detroit in the 1920s—persists. It's the rascally grins, captured in black-and-white photos, of gangsters leaning up against Ford Model Ts. It's the glitzy interiors of speakeasies, Josephine Baker belting out "Blue Skies," and Fats Waller insisting that he "Ain't Misbehavin'." I picture my grandmother in a dropped-waist dress with a fringe, beads double strung and hanging low, and a scarf tied tightly around her head. My grandfather wears a double-breasted suit and a fedora, and he's smoking a cigar. In my imagination, she's like Zelda Fitzgerald, and he, Al Capone.

Several years ago, a writers' conference brought me to Detroit for the first time. Every evening, my fellow attendees and I were ushered into buses and delivered to cultural sites in the city. Our local hosts seemed to be showing off—or, perhaps, trying to convince us of—Detroit's potential to rise from the rubble and become a world-class city again.

I loved the city and the people I met while I was there. A cab driver gushing about recent improvements to the infrastructure. A hipster bookstore owner bragging about Elmore Leonard and Charles Bukowski and Detroit's rich literary history. A gritty bar owner telling stories about The White Stripes and garage rock. The spectacular Diego Rivera murals at the Detroit Institute of Art. And so much more.

It is a city full of incongruity. Superbly renovated buildings line one city block, then, a moment later, there are structures that look as if a giant has ripped away entire façades to root clumsily around inside. Collapsed staircases linger in the remnants of brick tenement houses. Filthy mattresses hang off fire escapes. Steel rail tracks, on which horse-drawn streetcars once glided, are buried in the street, long out of use. There are countless vacant lots, some strewn with debris and garbage, and others transformed into neatly cultivated gardens where tomatoes and eggplants and peppers grow to nourish the neighborhood.

It all seemed so broken, so chin-up hopeful to me. So ready for a win.

One evening, we were dropped off at the edge of the Heidelberg Project, an open-air, community art installation composed of abandoned houses, found objects, and many works created from unwanted things. The project's website states, "As a whole, the [Heidelberg Project] is symbolic of how many communities in Detroit have become discarded. It asks questions and causes the viewer to think. When you observe the [Heidelberg Project], what do you really see? Is it art? Is it junk? Is it telling a story?"[1]

Old, dilapidated homes are painted with enormous polka dots or decorated with huge, worn stuffed animals. There are strange iterations of the American flag painted on walls and fences and rough scraps of wood. Signs nailed to tree trunks lead our gazes up to objects placed high in the branches—toys, sometimes, or painted signs with impenetrable messages about war or God or the USA. Broken, naked Barbie dolls are nailed to the siding of one house. Dozens of vacuum cleaners stand together in a field like a military unit, rubber gloves pulled over their handles.

Our hosts distributed mint juleps in small plastic cups as we walked from exhibit to exhibit. The drinks were far too sweet and strong for me; I left mine on what I hoped was a trash bin. Walking around the Heidelberg Project was like peeking into a storage closet of my unconscious—chaotic, playful, and unnerving, ready to set the stage for bizarre and mystical dreams. I fought back uneasy giggles.

But then I saw a piece of work that stopped me short. Sitting on its own, on a patch of grass, was a sculpture constructed from a television set and other old appliance parts. On it were painted the words "Yahweh Meet Me Half Way." My awkward smile faded, and I found myself in tears standing before it. Somehow those words tore right into me and articulated a longing I hadn't yet found the words to express. I stood still as my group moved on.

Yahweh Meet Me Half Way.

I was in my early forties (was I halfway through life?) and craving a sign—some divine reassurance—that I was on the right track. I'd built an entire adult life—was growing a marriage, raising four children, creating a network of friendships, and my career as a writer and editor had begun to mature. But what did it all mean? I wondered whether my life would come together into a meaningful body of work, or whether it all was mishmash, just a bunch of discarded junk at a garage sale. A messy pile of clothing. A dirty white extension cord. A few paperback books. Some water-damaged magazines. All as chaotic and hodgepodge as these unlikely art installations in the middle of this city. Would the many jumbled pieces and false starts and carefully tended relationships of my life come together to compose a story worth telling? Was I, like the broken-down, chin-up hopeful city of Detroit, teetering on the edge of rebirth—or was I just headed for further decline?

Time seemed to be passing so quickly all of a sudden. When I turned forty, my first child was beginning middle school, and all four of my kids seemed as if they were passengers on a high-speed train through adolescence. I struggled to make the transition into parenting my tween and teenaged children. They were no longer bright-faced and hopeful, home every Friday night and delighted by "Make Your Own Pizza Night!" or trips to the library or family bike rides. Worse, the number of opportunities they had to upend their lives terrified me.

Tweens and teens don't understand how much parents long for them to be safely on the other side of this white-water raft adventure we call adolescence. Every story of a good kid falling in with the wrong friends or giving up on school or otherwise finding his or her way into trouble or danger makes a parent's heart clench. It's not that we think our kids are reckless or weak or unreliable, but we know that their brains are still developing and they won't be truly mature for a few more years. We know something they can't seem to grasp in earlier adolescence: life can change course very quickly. And we know how fragile it can be. Over and over, we hear stories of teenagers experimenting with drugs or being pressured into other risky behaviors, and sometimes a bad decision costs them their lives . . . or at least derails their dreams—and the dreams their parents had for them.

There seems to be a sea change when sixth grade begins—for children as well as for their parents. A recent study of American mothers found that mothers of children in middle school report the highest levels of "stress, loneliness and emptiness, and also the lowest levels of life satisfaction and fulfillment." Mothers of infants and adults were the most satisfied, but mothers of children in middle school "fare most poorly."[2] These findings fit my experience.

When each of my kids was in middle school and transitioning into puberty, with its attendant sullen moods and horniness and throbbing acne and grand intellectual leaps and growing separate identities, my own body was changing too. The baggers at the grocery store had, seemingly overnight, traded "miss" for "ma'am" when they addressed me. "Ma'am" made me feel invisible. A fortysomething suburban woman with scraggly gray hair at my temples, haunting the background of everyone else's lives. (Why do all men just get called "sir," while "miss" is used for cute young "thangs" and "ma'am" for us more matronly types?) Now a "ma'am," I was reminded of the line from one of my favorite movies, *High Society*, when Celeste Holm's Elizabeth Imbrie, on being given the decidedly ambivalent compliment that she is "quite a girl," says to Frank Sinatra's character, "I guess I must be getting either booky, hippy, or toothy." I was now all three.

I wondered if I could grow stronger and braver in this new part of life or if I would simply keep losing steam and muscle mass. I was in what a researcher has called that "tapering-off time, the perimenopausal decade"[3] between my reproductive years and menopause, though I'd only just begun to realize it. I felt tired. My skin was getting dry, and my heels cracked. I had odd bruises on my ankles that looked like someone had smeared colored chalk dust there. I had hot flashes and erratic moods and newly severe and unpredictable menstrual cycles. I bought a magnifying mirror and stared at my face with disbelief. What was with those enormous pores, and that Picassoesque scribble of broken blood vessels near my nose?

My early forties held other losses, too. My sister died. Fractures in my extended family cracked wide open, dividing us. The culture wars that continue to slash my country in half—our conflicting opinions about marriage equality, immigration, the environment, and other issues—seeped into a few of my friendships, straining them. I found myself in tricky social situations that, despite my best efforts, I could not make better.

And I second-guessed myself professionally. My dream job of writing a column for a major newspaper was gone in a flash when the paper fired all its freelance columnists. I moved on and began to write books, but was anyone even reading them? My first book came out at the same time as the novel *Fifty Shades of Grey*; and that book—unlike mine—was *everywhere*. Its success mocked my efforts as a writer; lascivious quotes in print ads and great stacks of *Fifty Shades* smacked their wet lips at me every time I turned around. Was writing trashy erotica the only way to win in an industry that itself seemed destined for obscurity? When my royalty statements arrived, I fed them, unopened, to the shredder.

In college, I'd studied cultural anthropology and very nearly went on to grad school in the field. Before my husband and I had kids, I tapped into that background by working for a global health organization. Ever besieged by wanderlust, I loved trav-eling abroad to visit public health clinics and to work in foreign cities, but mostly I cherished the sense of purpose I had in my work. I saw firsthand how medical interventions and micro-loans and vaccines saved the lives of people in some of the world's lowest income countries. But it had been decades since I'd had the chance to dig deeply into this kind of work. Would I ever be able to return to it, or was I destined to remain in the pleasant custody of the suburbs, standing in the grocery store aisle weighing the relative merits of different brands of dryer sheets and juice boxes?

One of my kids' favorite movies when they were little was *Chitty Chitty Bang Bang*, and it was not only the spine-chilling character of the Child Catcher that unsettled me. In the movie, Dick Van Dyke plays the middle-aged, graying, and somewhat loopy Caractacus Potts, an unsuccessful inventor. After years of creating oddball devices, he is granted twenty seconds with someone who could bring one of his inventions to market. Potts botches the meeting, and the annoyed business owner dismisses him, saying, "Too late. Had your chance. Muffed it."

Was I as pathetic and half-baked a figure as Potts?

Had I "muffed" all the opportunities life had handed me?

What unsettled me the most, however, was that I was strain-ing to keep my faith. Why didn't God feel closer to me at this point in life? Shouldn't I feel *more* certain, and not less, about the presence of a loving God? I longed for purpose, for vision, for some small nod that would let me know that I was on the right track. I prayed anxious, grabby prayers in the middle of the night. *Am I missing something? Am I doing anything right? Are you there, God? It's me, Jenni.*

The answer to my frantic prayers seemed to be silence. Not a companionable silence, but one as lonely and foreboding as a car door slamming, the sound echoing against the concrete walls of a deserted parking garage. I longed for a sure, clear sense that I wasn't wasting my life, frittering away my gifts, unplugged from what really mattered. Standing before that art installation at the Heidelberg Project, I felt stuck. I wondered for what felt like the hundredth time: Couldn't God or the universe or *someone* give me a sign?

Yahweh, hello?

Couldn't you just meet me *halfway*?

TWO

Jenny's (Better) Bio

The day my friend Jenny posted a new bio on her website, I was plunged into a pit of despair. A slough of despond. A crushing, if also temporary, identity crisis. Whether a slight hormonal upsurge (or downswing) had anything to do with it is anyone's guess. But on an otherwise ordinary Saturday afternoon, I started coming apart at the seams.

Jenny and I have been friends for more than twenty years. She's the kind of friend I can travel with and not interrupt our conversation by closing the bathroom door or slipping away to change my clothes. So yes, she's seen me in my granny underwear (as opposed to her much slinkier underthings). A professional yogi, she's strong and lithe—and, with her, I'll even put my most clumsy self on display, sweating profusely as I try to salute the sun or hold that plank just a few seconds longer.

Both of us married our college boyfriends and understand what it means to commit to another person for the long haul. We've fessed up about the particulars of our sex lives—including the way growing older has affected desire and pleasure . . .

and no, not for the worse. We talk about the tedious aspects of parenting, as well as the conversations, epiphanies, and incidents of true connection with our children that make all the mind-numbingly dull or exasperating moments worthwhile. Both of us are writers, and we seek each other out for encouragement when it feels as if we are just banging our fists on the keyboards, pounding out nothing of value. And when we show up for weekends away together, we arrive with the same provisions: brie, rice crackers, baby carrots, dark chocolate, fig jam, a bottle of prosecco.

As I stared at my computer screen, reading and rereading Jenny's new bio, my ego awoke, yawned, and stretched its arms wide, readying itself to thrash me with self-recrimination. Unlike my bio, Jenny's was so very right on. She had struck just the right balance of professional and funny. Mine was a bore. The funniest thing in it was a reference to my stint as the writer of the local police blotter, reporting on minor infractions including garden gnome thefts. (Seriously.) I was suddenly quite certain that I was a vapid, dull, wholly skippable person. I felt a wave of shame. *Who am I, anyway?* Just a middle-aged mother of four teenagers who, many days, didn't seem to appreciate me very much.

Timothy Keller says the ego is always ready to prepare its "self-esteem résumé." Its natural condition is "empty, painful, busy, and fragile."[1] Yes, yes, yes, and yes. After reading Jenny's new bio, my ego was on a rampage. What was I doing with my life? Had I ever written anything that mattered? Why was I so "soft in the middle" when the rest of my life was so hard?[2] That I knew better than to do this to myself only made things worse. I scolded myself: Was a well-written bio really a litmus test for whether my life had value? Was I not finally above this sort of thing, for crying out loud?

A few years ago, I went to a close friend's birthday dinner in New York City. I'd never before met the three other people who came that night. One was in the traveling cast of a Broadway musical. Another was an actor who had just returned from California after doing a guest spot on a TV show. My friend and the other guest, a college professor, were just beginning to date. They eyed each other sweetly, occasionally reaching across the table to touch the other's forearms. (It was adorable.)

After we chatted for about half an hour, the conversation turned to me. When asked about my life, I fumbled over my words. *Freelance writer. Parenting books. Adoption. Chicago suburbs. Four children. At-home mom.* I sounded like a one-dimensional 1950s housewife—June Cleaver talking about housework or fretting over the Beav's shenanigans, primly patting her hands dry at the kitchen sink.

As I stammered, my friend jumped in. "She's mom to my favorite kids in the world," she said. "And I love her work."

The others looked on, their smiles wan. They regarded me cautiously now, as though they knew something I didn't . . . as though I was about to receive a diagnosis for some incurable disease.

"Four children. *Wow,*" one woman said, her voice flat, finally breaking the silence. "That's a lot."

After another moment that seemed to last two hours, someone changed the subject. I didn't say much for the rest of the night. I felt chastised—by these strangers and by myself—for having such a dreary, plain vanilla life. I'd also lived in New York years ago, had a professional life and a close group of friends there. But twenty years after leaving the city, I wondered if I'd become a sort of caricature of myself, padding around my house in my stocking feet, scribbling notes about motherhood into my journal, putting my kids' soccer games on the calendar, and wondering what to make for dinner. Had I become a walking cliché?

And then, years later, there I was being held captive again by throbbing insecurity after reading Jenny's bio.

Marcia Reynolds, an author and executive coach, describes what emotionally chaotic moments like these can accomplish in women's lives. "Sometimes you have to lose yourself to find yourself," she writes. "Some call this a mid-life crisis; I call it the Heroine's Journey."

"It is okay to lose your equilibrium when others think your life should be smooth sailing. It is okay to question your life's purpose. It's okay to say, 'I don't know who I am,'" Reynolds writes. "It is better to ask the questions and seek the answers than to live a numb life."[3]

After reading Jenny's new bio, I felt anything but numb. I decided that although it was too late for tap dancing and singing lessons or for a flashy and braggable professional life on stage or in some other career, I *could* work to craft a snappy bio. That, at least, seemed like a reasonable task for a Saturday afternoon.

I texted Jenny. "I hate my bio. Your new one is great. I don't know myself well enough to write anything good."

"Yeah, right," she responded. She likes me too much to know how serious I was, and it seemed my desperation hadn't translated via text. I was vaguely aware that I was being irrational, but crafting a new bio now obsessed me.

Years ago, my friend Anthony told me that one of the things he and I have in common is how well we keep our "crazy" under wraps, like magma under deep-pile carpet. I was aware that it wasn't under wraps at that moment; it was boiling and bubbling up. Jotting ideas in my notebook, I walked around my office pulling books from the shelves, flipping them over, reading cleverly worded author profiles. Everyone else's bios—rich with accomplishment—struck at my core. I decided that the only way I could overcome my fate of becoming a complete wash up—wearing ill-advised chunky necklaces and jeggings, no doubt—was writing a bio that would impress even my dining companions from that mortifying night in New York.

An hour later, I gave up. Everything I scratched into my notebook came out forced, phony. I tried to distract myself. I started the laundry, swept the back porch, and loaded the dishwasher. Bringing in the mail, I found a review copy of a new book with a note from a publicist asking me to consider endorsing it. I looked around, defending myself to my imagined crowd of detractors.

See? They want me to endorse this. I'm *someone.*

A thought shot back. *So what? You write too many endorsements anyway.* I thought of the Elinor Lipman essay in which she defends her rather impressive catalog of blurbs. Like Lipman, I get multiple requests for book endorsements every month and, like her, when I receive a review copy, I lean toward writing a blurb. "We're all in this together," I think. But it would be a lie to say that writing blurbs is pure altruism; my ego gets a shot in the arm when I'm asked to do it. I *like* seeing my name on other people's book covers, and I'm pleased when I get a note from a friend saying her book club is reading a book with one of my blurbs on the back.

See? I'm someone, my ego shouts.

"Word gets around in editorial circles, so blurb ubiquity begets more padded envelopes," Lipman writes in her essay "Confessions of a Blurb Slut."[4]

You're *a blurb slut*, my inner critic hissed that afternoon.

I set the envelope aside and emptied the fruit bowl, tossed out a shriveled lime, and artfully rearranged the apples and pears and plums. Unaware of what had been spinning in my mind that day, my husband approached, holding his iPad.

"We need to update your frequent flier account," he said, turning the screen toward me. "Pick three security questions."

I rifled through the kitchen junk drawer for a pair of reading glasses, then sat down with him at the kitchen counter.

What is your favorite ice cream?

What is the first big city you visited?

What color was your house growing up?

What is your favorite movie?

Who is your favorite artist?

I was flung deep into a well of anxiety once again. "These are hard," I said, taking off my glasses. "I just don't know."

David eyed me warily. "Favorite ice cream?" he asked.

"Well, I like bitter chocolate chip, but if I have more than a few bites, it's too much for me."

"So will you remember that answer?" he asked, typing. "'Bitter chip,' or do you call it 'bitter chocolate chip'?"

"Let's skip that one," I said.

"Okay, what's the first big city you visited?"

"I don't remember. You know my parents traveled a lot when I was little."

"What color was your childhood home?"

"It was yellow, but then they got blue siding. The siding was vinyl, maybe. No, wait. It was metal and kind of a grayish slate blue," I said. "And now it's gray. But I remember it best as that smoky blue."

"Jennifer." My husband only uses my full name when he's annoyed with me. He took a deep breath. "Let's move on: Who is your favorite artist?"

"Musical? Visual? What type of art?" I felt tears rising in my eyes and cleared my throat. "These are hard. Don't you think these questions are hard?"

"Van Gogh," he said, typing. "I'm going to say Van Gogh."

"I really love Georgia O'Keeffe," I whispered. "I mean, if we're going with visual art. Or Rothko."

He groaned.

In the end, David chose the questions as well as the answers, and he took a screenshot. "I'll hang on to this," he said, hurrying from the room, leaving me standing in the kitchen wiping away tears.

I didn't blame him for being puzzled. You'd think by age forty-three these answers would have come more easily to me, but that day, they simply pointed a glaring spotlight at how disconnected I felt from myself. When I was a child, I loved to shoot off a list of my favorites—favorite color, animals, books, and—yes—favorite flavor of ice cream. Where did that easy self-awareness and confidence go? I wondered if it was inevitable that, after raising kids for more than a decade, I'd start to lose myself, forget what made me smile, what tasted good to me, how I really wanted to spend my days.

I decided to take yet another pass at revising my bio. I opened my notebook, grabbed a pen, and logged on to Twitter to read super-short iterations of the professional bio. Here I was met with more cleverness and shining achievement that seemed to cast my own sense of self further into the shadows.

Actress Molly Ringwald's Twitter bio read: "Actress, writer, singer, mother, your former teen-age crush."

Oh great. I forgot to become a movie star, and now I'd nothing witty to write about myself. Too late now.

Tom Hanks: "I'm that actor in some of the movies you liked and some you didn't. Sometimes I'm in pretty good shape, other times I'm not. Hey you gotta live, you know?"

Anna Kendrick: "Pale, awkward and very very small. Form an orderly queue, gents. Location: probably by the food."

Dang it. I was reminded that not only was I not a movie star; I couldn't even do the "Cups" song from *Pitch Perfect*.

I wondered how I got to this place where I was completely self-absorbed, where I'd lost all perspective, comparing my life and accomplishments to A-list celebrities. What in the world was wrong with me? My ego was out of control, shouting, "Pick me, pick me, pick me!" and desperately grasping for an improved self-esteem resume. I realized I was in tears again.

Sitting on the edge of my bed, I reached for Timothy Keller's *The Freedom of Self-Forgetfulness*, a sanity-bringer of a book that I've returned to many times over the years when I find myself out of emotional or spiritual whack. The book is one of my life's companions, a trusted and supportive friend. It has taken up permanent residence on my bedside table.

In it, Keller points out that a distinctive about the Christian religion—of which I am a lifelong, if often inept, practitioner—is that the final verdict is in before we do anything. The ruling has been made: we are loved beyond all comprehension. We never need to prove ourselves worthy to God or anyone else. So if "the court is adjourned," as Keller says, and we have nothing to prove, we can get distance from that grabby, insatiable ego.

True humility, Keller writes, "means I stop connecting every experience, every conversation, with myself. In fact, I stop thinking about myself. The freedom of self-forgetfulness. The blessed rest that only self-forgetfulness brings."[5]

I walked downstairs and found David sorting through the mail. He eyed me guardedly, wondering whether the emotional wave I had been riding would come crashing into him again.

"Let's get the kids and bike downtown," I said. "Let's get out of the house, get some ice cream."

He agreed.

A half hour later, at the ice cream parlor, we were in a long line, crammed together in the small space. I scanned the buckets through the glass. David ordered pistachio. Two of my kids got cookie dough, and my younger daughter ordered something that looked like an exploding Care Bear. Then it was my turn. I knew what I wanted, but I almost didn't want to say it.

"And you, miss?" the boy behind the counter asked. (Miss, not ma'am. I liked that. He'd get a big tip.)

"Vanilla," I said. "Just plain vanilla."

Outside on the sidewalk, I snapped a picture of my ice cream cone and texted it to Jenny. "My new/old fave."

"Jealous," she responded.

Several years later, I text Jenny. "Wrote about you in the new book. I can change your name, blur your details. Emailing it to you now. Let me know."

"Will read tonight," she responds.

The next morning, I find a note from Jenny in my inbox:

Okay. So the ironic (and hilarious) thing about this chapter is that I wrote my bio, sitting on the Highline, during one of the most miserable summers of my life. Cranky kids, hottest NYC summer on record since 1800s, lots of relatives shacking up under our very hot roof for three weeks. I was in a fit of career despair and panic precipitated by trying to get my bio done. It was late, and I had been avoiding it, feeling I had nothing to show for twenty years worth of chipping away at various "careers," and I had just read your list of published work and I felt like I didn't belong in the club . . . so I decided to make my bio quirky and clever, as a cover for having nothing real to include!

Reading Jenny's email, I have to laugh—at both of us. *Career despair. Panic. Didn't belong in the club.* Of course I understand exactly what she was feeling those years ago. It was I, after all, who got myself tangled up in knots and who spent hours trying to make my own life and work sound more impressive than it was. But now both Jenny and I, a few years further down the line, are feeling more settled, more accepting of what it is we've done with our time as we've chipped away at twenty years of raising children, nurturing marriages, deepening friendships, and, yes, growing as writers. Happily, as Keller says, we've come to accept—most days, at least—that "the court is adjourned," and we have nothing to prove.

THREE

Middle-Aged Is Actually a Thing

Growing up, I was a faculty kid. My mother taught in the graduate school at the college in my hometown, and my summers were spent overseas in the United Kingdom and elsewhere in Europe, tagging along with my mom and her grad students on an annual summer study program. Perks included learning to drink good coffee in the Netherlands as a child, prompting a lifelong love affair with very strong brew. I went people-watching in London's Regent's Park, where I was fascinated by the innocent ease with which men stripped down to their undies and women pulled off their tops to sunbathe over their lunch hours. And, as helicopter parenting hadn't been invented yet, I loved the freedom to explore unfamiliar cities on my own. Those summers abroad gave me—for better and worse—a lingering case of wanderlust, and they are at least partly responsible for making me a reader; I spent many afternoons browsing in bookstores and reading at the back of a classroom during my mother's lectures.

Most summers, I made a friend or two from the group of students and, as I got older, I'd harbor secret crushes on some of the men. (Kindly, they pretended not to notice.) By the time I was in high school, I'm not proud to confess, I had come to view my mother's women students with some contempt. That they were often in their forties (or older), and that they were returning to school seemed sad to me. Sad, as in *pathetic*. Wasn't the point to be *done* with school by the time you were in your early twenties so you could, I don't know, get on with being a real grown-up? I don't remember what I pictured that would look like. Champagne wishes and caviar dreams, maybe? So why, all those years after finishing college, would a person go *backward*? That the women students were typically unmarried also offended my sixteen-year-old sensibilities. Single, a bit worn out, wearing pleated, baggy acid-washed jeans, fanny packs, and cardigans with shoulder pads, they often carried extra weight around their middles, and their gray roots showed.

Inside my adolescent mind, it seemed as if these women had lost the thread of whatever it was they *really* wanted to do, so they gave up and "just" went back to school. Hadn't they been able to figure out who they were before then? What was their *problem*? Although I'd read Tolkien, I wouldn't yet connect to his brilliant line "Not all those who wander are lost."[1] I can just see myself turning away from one of my mother's students, dropping a root beer–flavored Lip Smacker into my Bermuda bag, and clapping the wooden handles together with disgust.

"As *if!*"

C. S. Lewis wrote that pride is the "one vice of which no man in the world is free; which everyone loathes when he sees it in someone else."[2] And indeed pride does, as they say, go before a fall. My own fall would come some twenty-five years later.

My teenage daughter and I are driving around on errands, listening to the radio, and chatting about her school day when— with the swift surprise of a summer thunderstorm—her mood clouds over and she declares that she needs something to eat. Something "drive-through." Something *now*.

Minutes later, the storm has passed, and she hands me one of her fries.

"Try this," she says. "Way too salty, right?"

"Oh," I say, my lips tingling. "I like them that way."

"That's because you're *old*," she says.

"I'm not *old*." I try to keep my voice pleasant but firm. "I'm *middle-aged*."

She dissolves into almost hiccupping laughter and then catches her breath. "There is no such thing as *middle-aged*," she says. "There's only *old* and *young*. Thirty is young; thirty-five is old."

"Thirty-five!"

"But don't worry," she pats my arm. "Old isn't a bad thing. It means more wiseness."

"Wisdom," I say. My words come out more sharply than I intend.

She just laughs: "Sorry, grammar police!"

We fall back into easy conversation, and I realize, probably not for the very first time, but with more clarity than ever before, that I'm decidedly middle-aged. I suppose I've been trying to ignore it, hoping it's not noticeable to anyone else. Like when you catch your reflection in the mirror and see a bit of spinach in your teeth. You wonder how long it's been there, and you rake back over every interaction you've had since lunch, hoping against hope that somehow no one has spotted it. But now I see myself through my daughter's eyes, as I accidentally belt out the wrong lyrics to her favorite song.

To my daughter, I'm like those students of my mother's. A little lost, a little lumpy, a little out of it. *Old.* I was stingy with those women years ago, judging their life choices, the fact that they were single, and—ugh—those pleated jeans. I saw them as caricatures. Remembering this, I feel a rush of appreciation for my daughter's usual graciousness, even at her age. She still snuggles in close beside me when we watch a movie together. She laughs (or LOLs, at least) when I send her what I think is a funny text. And, when I ask for it, she gives me a final once-over when I'm dressed to go out. "Not those clogs. The boots," she says. "Otherwise, it's all good." In short, she is kind to me, even if she thinks that, as a woman over thirty-five, I'm old.

My mother's students, I imagine, didn't feel old either. Maybe they hoped that no one was noticing their transition into middle age—that proverbial bit of spinach in their teeth—or judging them for the extra pounds they carried or wondering why they were unmarried. Maybe my judgment wasn't as undetectable as I hope it was, and they had to sigh, knowing my time would come. My daughter, when she is my age, won't feel old either. She'll have her own people and plans and perceived flaws and obvious gifts. I hope she'll have rich memories and a hopeful faith that will help her endure the losses and burdens of her own life. And on and on it goes. Ecclesiastes 1:9 reads, "History merely repeats itself. It has all been done before. Nothing under the sun is truly new."

We pull into the driveway, and my daughter leans in close and looks in my eyes. "That was fun," she says. "Thanks for everything."

I manage to land a kiss to the side of her head before she pulls away, slips out of the car, and hurries into the house. She has homework to do, friends to call, new clothes to stash away in her room. Tomorrow—or in ten minutes—she might be annoyed with me, seeing me as that odd, awkward mom who somehow has lost all the magic I held when she was younger. For now, I'm grateful that she loves me as I am, gray roots and all.

FOUR

Shut-Door Panic

The word *midlife* is often spoken as though it were the setup for a joke. It's as if we middle-aged people are laughable, mere shells of our former selves, caricatures with our Botox and bikeathons, convertibles and comfort shoes, spray tans and Spanx. Women are told what "not to wear" once we hit forty, including—but not limited to—skinny jeans, lip liner, and miniskirts. Oh, and fishnet stockings. (Really? *Fishnets*? Who even wore those in their twenties? I know I didn't, except one Halloween in college when I dressed as Madonna. The stockings were key; it was the "Like a Virgin" era.) Men aren't spared these kinds of messages either. After forty, they're told to stop wearing backward baseball caps, old concert T-shirts, leather bomber jackets, and white socks in public.

People in midlife are often depicted as clumsy and distracted, forever fumbling with our reading glasses and bumbling the remote control. Our lips are pursed and our purses empty. (Bet you didn't know that "empty purse" is a euphemism for the post-menopausal uterus.) We're suckers for every new diet

craze (kale! quinoa! clean eating!), and some of us start running marathons in desperate attempts to chase away a growing
awareness of our own mortality. Middle-aged men are emascu-
lated—exactly how many jokes can be made about beer bellies,
prostate problems, and erectile dysfunction? TV sitcoms and
raunchy birthday cards (scan the "Turning 40" section of the
greeting card display) love summing us up in these ways. Sure,
some of these stereotypes hit dangerously close to home, but
aren't the middle-aged people you know more complicated and
interesting than that?

Midlife can also be spoken as the first breath of the phrase
midlife crisis. If you look for the etymology of the term, you'll
be directed to the German word *Torschlusspanik*. This is translated into English as "shut-door panic," or the fear of being on
the wrong side of a closing door. In the satirical *Ladybird Book
of the Mid-Life Crisis*, the first page reads: "When we are young,
we all dream of doing something wonderful and exciting with
our lives. What will we be? A cosmonaut? An underwater de-
tective? A tommy gunner? . . . Anything is possible. And then,
one day, it isn't."[1]

Ouch.

As I approached forty, doors were indeed closing around
me. My kids would be out of the house in a few years. Had I
taught them everything I'd meant to? What had they learned
about creating and sustaining a marriage from watching my
husband and me so closely day after day, year after year?
Would the experience of living under the same roof for eighteen years fortify each of our relationships for the rest of our
lives? I felt stings of regret about trips I'd always fantasized we
might make as a family. When the kids were small, vacation
possibilities seemed endless, but then, suddenly, the time to
take them was almost up. (Oh, and the first tuition payment for

college was coming due.) I wondered what values and convictions they would choose to keep from this intense first part of their lives. Would they remain in the faith in which they were raised? And when my mind flickered on the image of dropping any one of them off at college, I felt crushing pain in my chest. After focusing on every detail of raising, feeding, and nurturing these four people, how could I simply walk away, leaving them behind, one after the other in neat two-year intervals, in their freshman dorms? Was there any way to prepare my heart for those inevitable heartbreaks?

After her younger child left for college, one corporate executive, a devoted mother, admitted, "I sometimes feel as though a part of my heart has been ripped out of my chest. After all those years of purposeful and fierce mothering, always managing to put my children first in spite of my career, I have been surprised at how very physical and painful this loss feels."[2]

All that I'd said yes to in my adult life—marriage, work, church and other volunteer commitments, and the "purposeful and fierce mothering" to which I'd also devoted myself—had, of course, meant saying no to other things. Had I turned right when I should have gone left? And how do you know when you're in "midlife," anyway? Was I halfway through?

I started doing basic arithmetic around my fortieth birthday.

$$\begin{array}{r} 40 \\ + \ 40 \\ \hline 80 \end{array}$$

$$\begin{array}{r} 44 \\ + \ 44 \\ \hline 88 \end{array}$$

$$46$$
$$+\ 46$$
$$92$$

What constituted a full life? Eighty? Eighty-eight? Did I really *want* to live to ninety-two? Where did the years go between thirty and forty-five? (Oh, right. I had my head down, busy in the tasks of raising children.)

Shut-door panic indeed.

But actually, most of us "do" midlife without crisis. A ten-year study debunked the idea that midlife crisis is prevalent in America. Researchers concluded that only about 10 percent of Americans experience a true "midlife crisis," characterized by powerful discontent with their marriages, regret about their general health, and yearning to be young again.[3] Maybe it's less like a crisis and more like a slog through a period of low-level unease, regardless of whether we are married or have children, as we make our way into this new stage in life. It's a happier stage, for many of us, once we get our bearings. In the thick of midlife, we, for the large part, keep our commitments, find ourselves coming into our own professionally, and mature into the people we always hoped we would be.

Yes, but there's turbulence when we make our descent and landing here. Our families change. Parents have to buck up and say those wrenching goodbyes to their kids. We have new responsibilities and concerns for our aging parents. We *are* mortal and *will* die someday—creaky knees, thinning hair, and deepening wrinkles remind us on a daily basis.

But *crisis*?

Juliette Binoche, who seems to me to be too talented and elegant ever to worry about aging, beautifully described what it's like to grow older. "On the one hand you're becoming more fragile and on the other hand there's a strength that comes with it," she said in an interview.

Asked to clarify "more fragile," Binoche said: "Well, physically you're changing so it makes you more fragile. Simple as that. There's something else that's coming. . . . You have to overcome certain things; the need of power, the need of possession, the need of enjoyment—which are really the big three things that the human being has to face at a certain point. It's challenging, it's very challenging, but I think when you really make a decision to overcome it there's a freedom that comes with it and it's quite enjoyable."[4]

Feeling the impulse to be intentional about *enjoying* this new decade, I decided to put my best foot forward when I approached forty. "I want a party," I told my husband. "A big one. A *bash*."

He and I got to work. We sampled bottles of pinot noir and chardonnay at our local wine shop and ordered cases of the ones we liked best. We sent invitations to a hundred of our favorite friends. We hired a string quartet. David's brother and his wife flew in from Boston, and the day of the party, my sister-in-law and I bought armloads of flowers at the grocery store—daisies and purple wax flowers—and she made centerpieces using dollar-store glass vases and orange curling ribbon. Caterers brought fruit, cheese and crackers, and appetizers and arranged them on tables in my church hall. That night, my friends showered me with kindness. A few gave lovely speeches. The food was simple and good. It all was just as I'd hoped it would be, and I felt like the poster child for a "Life Begins at Forty" campaign.

Fast-forward five years to a much smaller birthday celebration. I called it my "Halfway to Ninety" party, and about twenty friends gathered in my home. By then, some of the friendships I'd thought would see me through the next part of my life had shriveled up, died on the vine, and fallen to the ground. This, I learned, happens to many of us in our forties. We lose track of some of the friends we get to know in the context of our kids' schools or playing fields. Or we find ourselves growing out of friendships. Other friends move. Some, inexplicably, ghost away.

Looking around at the guests at my "half ninety" party, I knew I wasn't the same person I'd been five years before. None of us were. But there we stood, aware in new ways of what it meant to be the grown-ups. We knew we had every reason to be grateful. One friend had nearly lost her life to cancer in those intervening years. Another had weathered a long season of unemployment. Another had divorced. Many of us had steered through some very choppy seas with our adolescent children. We were more wrinkled but wiser than we'd been five years earlier. And we were aware of how lucky we were to have each other.

And the years continue to flip by, each speedier than the last. I'll be fifty in a year. The little son who so sweetly played his cello at my fortieth birthday party just started his third year of college. This year, his younger brother graduated from high school and moved on to college as well. Although my heart was experienced with this kind of goodbye, this one had its own peculiar grief. With the first, in the weeks after he began college, missing him felt like an ever-present boulder pressing down on my chest. In time, that heaviness lifted, bit by bit by tiny bit. I felt more sanguine with the second, knowing I'd been through it before, telling myself that although I'd miss him, our relationship—like the one I have with his brother—is strong. There's nothing to fret about, I told myself. *Tra-la!*

But still, the loss was determined to make itself known. The weekend after taking my younger son to college, I stopped by the grocery store, feeling optimistic, organized, ready for the week ahead. All was well. Then a young couple came around the corner ahead of me, their toddler son sitting up front in the shopping cart, chattering to himself. The parents were focused on their list and checking the unit price of whatever they dropped into the cart. It was a perfectly ordinary moment in their lives, but, seeing them, a wave of grief washed over me. My face flushed and I felt physically ill. I steered my cart over to the side of the aisle and pretended to look at a box of pasta. "Ah, so there you are, Grief," I said to myself. The little family walked out of sight and, after a minute or two, my nausea passed. I wiped away my tears, took a deep breath, and continued on through the store.

In four short years, my husband and I will be empty nesters. Our two daughters will be gone, grown, off discovering the people and purposes that will shape their adult lives. As much as my heart will strain sometimes, and feel as if it just might tear apart with missing my children, this is all as it should be. I expect I'll feel a knotty mix of envy and compassion when I spend time with friends who came to parenthood later in life, whose chronological middle age (the aches! the pains! the prostate problems!) and their roles as parents of young children overlap. When they are taking children to school concerts or dressing them up for Halloween, I'll be sending a care package to a dorm or texting one of my kids, just to check in. I expect my friends with little ones will look at empty nesters like my husband and me—maybe after an excruciatingly long night with a sick child or hard afternoon with a middle schooler—and it will feel incomprehensible that their children will *ever* grow up and leave home. But then, inevitably, there will come a day when they too will find themselves on the other side of a closing door, and they might find themselves panicking, wondering how the time could have possibly passed so quickly.

FIVE

Coyotes and Shadow Selves

The last time I'd seen him was on curriculum night at the high school. He leaned back in his chair, his feet crossed on the top of his desk. He was a veteran teacher who spoke indulgently about his own quirks—a stuffed animal collection, a fondness for a certain kind retro candy (I think it was NECCO Wafers), and so on. High school students found his classes engaging, and many considered him a friend.

In his post-arrest mug shot, however, I see a different iteration of the man. His face is pale, his eyes wide, and his eyebrows are jerked upward in an almost comic expression of terror. Was it the threat of almost half a century of prison time that altered him so drastically? The shock of the neon orange jumpsuit? Or was it that, in the moment his relationship with one of his students had been discovered, *something else* had been exposed, something he'd spent a lifetime working hard to hide? Carl Jung called it the "Shadow," and he said that when we repress it, it can "burst forth" with a vengeance.

"Unfortunately there can be no doubt that man is, on the whole, less good than he imagines himself or wants to be," Jung wrote. "Everyone carries a Shadow, and the less it is embodied in the individual's conscious life, the blacker and denser it is. . . . At all events, it forms an unconscious snag, thwarting our most well-meant intentions."[1]

Imagine the gathering of foreboding thunderheads that blocked the better angels of this man's nature when, over the course of a year, he met a sixteen-year-old student for sex in parking lots, in classrooms, and in his home. These encounters were later cataloged in obscene detail by the local news media. Public outcry in our community was, of course, deafening. The stories were almost pornographic. We were shocked, heartbroken for the girl whom he abused and for her family, and disgusted by his crimes. *He said he was a Christian! He betrayed the whole community's trust! He raped a minor!*

As awful as this news was, sometimes I found myself wondering whether we were outraged by something else, something in addition to the ugliness of his crimes. Could the fact that he presented himself as a clean-cut, "aw shucks" jokester with stories about the church choir while hiding a twisted, nefarious side prick our own consciences? Did his arrest uncomfortably remind us that we *all* have shadowy impulses, even when we look so very respectable from the outside? Were we reminded that, as Jung said, we *all* are less good than we imagine ourselves to be?

I wondered, after the man's arrest, how any of us can keep ourselves honest, keep our eyes open to our own flaws and brokenness—to our shadow selves—when it's so easy to conceal and ignore what is corrupt inside us. Richard Rohr writes, "I have prayed for years for one good humiliation a day, and then, I must watch my reaction to it. I have no other way of spotting both my denied shadow self and my idealized persona."[2] This seems a very brave request to make, a true surrender. Although I haven't incorporated this as a spiritual practice, I have learned to take note and stand back when I feel the sharp sting of an insult, when I feel I've been misunderstood, or when my pride is injured in some other way. My shadow might be summoned in a moment when I feel like I'm being taken for granted or when one of my kids is disrespectful or sullen. It's in those moments when I'm "offended" when my shadow gathers strength and looms large. It's humbling to admit that I can so quickly be thrown off-kilter and feel searing anger or pride spike in my heart, seemingly from out of nowhere. Just when I think I've "arrived" spiritually, something throws me, and I'm reminded how fragile I am. These moments are splashes of cold water in the face, jarring reminders that the ideal self I project is flimsy, an apparition. But these serve a purpose, reminding me of God's grace and prompting me to slow down and find my spiritual center again. "Not a single person on earth is always good and never sins," we are reminded in Ecclesiastes 7:20. Still, we like to fool ourselves into believing otherwise.

Of course, it's much easier to lead with my projected self. I like, for instance, to describe myself as someone who's great with kids and truly connects with them. I joke that, at a party, you can find me at the kids' table—and that's often the case. I love kids' senses of humor, their candor, and their delight. I'll do knock-knock jokes all day and am happy to talk nonsense, play endless games of tic-tac-toe, or sit cross-legged on the floor for hours, messing with LEGO sets or action figures. Every Easter, I invite several families for brunch and an egg hunt, and I try to exceed the kids' expectations year after year. I love that some of our youngest Easter guests have come to refer to me as "the Easter Egg Lady." And yes, I support charities that advocate for children, work to end to gender-based violence, and promote girls' education. But although all of this is true, and despite how affable and sympathetic it all sounds, it's a mistake for me to rest in the comfort of that constructed self.

Several years ago, my friend Jon Sweeney spoke at the adult Sunday school class at my church. I don't remember his topic, but I'm guessing it had to do with the spiritual friendship between Saint Francis and Saint Clare of Assisi, on which he's an expert. Somehow, our discussion of loving our neighbors and what it means to be part of the body of Christ slid into a critique of American parents' idolization of family. *Their* own— *our* own—nuclear families. Jon said, for instance, that many of us think nothing of driving the biggest, most indestructible military-grade vehicle around town so that, in a collision between our car and someone else's, our car will "win." With airbags and seat belts and a rock-solid construction, our own children, no matter how nasty the accident, won't get a scratch. But, Jon asked, in what way is that loving the neighbor who can't afford a car like that and is driving her family around in a small, lightweight vehicle? "In a crash, you win, and she loses," Jon said. "And probably loses big. But you don't question your choice or give it a second thought. Why? Because keeping your own children safe is all that matters to you."

Although I don't drive a five-ton truck, his comments stung my conscience. I asked myself in what ways did I *say* that I cared about the world's children, but so (over)prioritized the care and well-being of my *own* kids that I ignored the needs of those who live in poverty. In what ways did my choices contribute to the global warming that makes storms and droughts and other disasters more intense, thus causing more pain to children around the world? I had to face up to the fact that I'm just like that person in the proverbial bulletproof SUV, buckling up my children, filling the car with gas, loading the cup holders with cool bottles of water, and not acknowledging how my choices reverberate around the globe. I conveniently don't *prioritize* the well-being of *other people's* children . . . especially those whose names and faces I don't know and who live out of my sight. The day Jon spoke to our class, I loosened my grip on the cozy, concocted sense of self that I'd found so much pleasure in before—and I committed to looking more carefully at my choices, questioning the way I placed the comfort and well-being of my own family above that of others. Another brittle edge of my false self started flaking and peeling away. Again, it's a lifelong process of dismissing handy rationalizations, training my gaze onto neighbors who suffer in my community or around the world, and letting my prickly edges be worn down.

In her book *Dangerous Surrender: What Happens When You Say Yes to God*, Kay Warren tells the story of how she became an advocate for people affected by poverty and HIV/AIDS. Warren is the wife of Rick Warren, the well-known pastor and bestselling author. For years, she writes, she felt that her gifts were overlooked while her husband was ever in the spotlight. But ultimately, she found her calling. She writes, "I've found that discovering God's will often resembles looking at an undeveloped Polaroid photograph. When the camera spits out the picture, the images are gray and shapeless, but the longer you look at the picture, the clearer it becomes."[3]

But it's a challenge to let these images develop, and to be honest about what we see. In the bucolic suburbs, we have mastered the game face, ever promoting idealized versions of who we are. Facebook is an effective tool in this task, of course. We filter, curate, and carefully present versions of ourselves that are more attractive and altruistic than we often are. We tend to keep our sorrows secret: disintegrating marriages, vitriolic relationships with children, financial worry. We appreciate our neighbors' respect for our privacy, and we don't much like surprises. As often as possible, we will turn away and even run from images or experiences that make us look at the nastiest parts of humanity—institutional racism, the inequality that binds too many of our neighbors to poverty, and perhaps especially whatever is greedy in our own hearts. We are experts at avoiding that which disquiets us.

The problem is that to be unsettled is a *good* thing, spiritually speaking. Unpleasant surprises such as the high school teacher's sordid crimes remind me that there is something undomesticated within *me* too. Something that needs to accept healing and forgiveness, something that desperately yearns for love. Something that's greedy, small, and puts my own cravings and desires before the needs of anyone else. Something that loses perspective, is disordered, and as theologian Peter Rollins writes, actually "denies the resurrection" by ignoring those in pain or who live on the margins in my country and all over the world. Rollins writes in a blog:

> I deny the resurrection of Christ every time I do not serve at the feet of the oppressed, each day that I turn my back on the poor; I deny the resurrection of Christ when I close my ears to the cries of the downtrodden and lend my support to an unjust and corrupt system. However there are moments when I affirm that resurrection, few and far between as they are. I affirm it when I stand up for those who are forced to live on their knees, when I speak for those who have had their tongues torn out, when I cry for those who have no more tears left to shed.[4]

For the last few years, our tidy suburb has been wrestling with another type of wild thing: coyotes. We provide an ample food supply for them, especially at night: the small pets we allow to run freely in our yards. Many residents wish the county would destroy the coyotes, but officials refuse to act.

When coyotes appear, we're instructed to shout, clap our hands, and even throw things at them. A banner on the city's webpage promises that if we do these things, the coyotes will trot away. Without negative reinforcement, however, they will become more aggressive.

Things were different years ago when I lived in the city. While I never encountered a coyote when I lived in Brooklyn, I was much more accustomed to seeing the untamed parts of life and the effects of a system that marginalizes the weak or ill. Returning home from church on Sunday afternoons meant walking down uneven brick sidewalks, often catching a whiff of putrefying trash left on the street, kicking off a flyer that had stuck to my shoe, or hearing the schizophrenic rants of the man who frequented his favorite corner in my neighborhood.

Back then, I lived with the visceral reality of a heartbroken and sometimes filthy world. I could no more control with whom I'd interact than I could direct the wind that made the discarded plastic bags dance in the treetops. I was forced to integrate the words of the creeds I'd just professed in church on my walk home.

From the Book of Common Prayer, whose liturgy Episcopalians follow every week, we pray the baptismal covenant:

Celebrant: Will you seek and serve Christ in all persons, loving your neighbor as yourself?

People: I will, with God's help.

Celebrant: Will you strive for justice and peace among all people, and respect the dignity of every human being?

People: I will, with God's help.[5]

In the suburbs, I can smuggle my eucharistic afterglow home, protected in my climate-controlled minivan, like a sack of organic groceries. Ignoring what's grim and foul in myself or in the world around me, however, doesn't make things better. Instead, as Jung concluded, pretending that shadow selves and their coyote impulses don't exist only emboldens them.

The teacher's mug shot and the coyote warnings disturb me and wake me up spiritually. Sometimes I need only confess my depraved impulses and self-centeredness, whether using the prayer book's formal text or an improvised, silent plea, and they trot away. But there are moments too when I must stomp my feet, shout, and throw things in the direction of my shadowy self, to let it know I see it and to scare it off.

SIX

Jury Duty

On the full-length mirror that hung on the back of my bedroom door when I was a child was a small, round Sandra Boynton sticker. If you're a parent, you might be familiar with her board books for babies, such as *Pajama Time!* and *Barnyard Time!* My personal favorite is *Oh My Oh My Oh Dinosaurs!* (Ms. Boynton is fond of the exclamation mark!) I stood and stared into that mirror for long periods as a child, searching my eyes, trying to elicit some answers, hoping somehow to be able to free myself from whatever mood was keeping me captive. My feet began to tingle, buried in the thick green shag carpet. My knees locked. I'd glance up at the Boynton sticker, a little round totem featuring a sketch of a hippo, face turned to the side, standing alone in a patch of grass.

"Things are getting worse," it read. "Please send chocolate."

Unfortunately, it was my first mantra, almost a prayer, a childhood response to everything from a poor grade to conflict with a friend and even to my parents' divorce. "Things are getting worse. Please send chocolate," I'd whisper. Somehow, in this season of life, I find myself regressing back into childish, "Please send chocolate" kinds of prayers.

Some disappointments are professional. After completing what I'd thought was some of the best writing I've done and hitting "send," I'd felt a flush of adrenaline. *Maybe, just maybe, things are turning around for me,* I thought. *I'm finally coming into my own, maturing into the writer I always hoped I'd be.* Alas, a day or two later, I received an icy response from an editor. She offered two options: take a kill fee or start over. (I started over.)

My pride took a hit when only a few people showed up to one of my speaking engagements. There were eleven, to be precise, and three were members of my family and three were close friends. The sponsoring organization had said they expected the event was going to be "huge." They told me to bring boxes of my books to sell. The night of the event, one woman (of the five actual attendees) wandered up to say she wanted to buy a book but had forgotten her wallet. I told her to just take what she wanted.

At home, things felt off-kilter. My husband took a new job and had to travel out of town a few days almost every week. I started having trouble sleeping at night. One of my children suffered a betrayal by someone considered to be a very close friend. Worse, we started to clash over the situation. Sometimes my child wanted to talk about it; sometimes I was directed to be silent and act as though nothing had happened. I got the signals crossed, again and again, and we ended up tangled in conflict and hurt feelings. Another child veered dangerously close to making some exceptionally bad choices, choices that were cut off at the pass when—thank God—I came across a text message detailing them.

Three of the kids had pricey medical interventions. The dishwasher quit, prompting a monthlong (and expensive) comedy of errors during which time the space under the kitchen sink became an archeological dig—plumbing and electrical issues kept being unearthed and repaired. I was up late into the night, washing and drying dishes. I slid my credit card out of my wallet and handed it to the plumber, the electrician, and the dishwasher deliveryman. The washing machine stopped working. And, finally, my laptop performed a slow, dramatic death scene, its screen frozen as it waved goodbye to me with its swirling color wheel of despair.

Around the same time, I received what I think was the first letter I'd ever gotten from my father. I've only seen him half a dozen times or so since my parents divorced when I was a child. Over the years, I've gotten occasional email messages, usually copied to a dozen or so other people whose names aren't familiar to me. A joke. An announcement about his professional life. A bit of health news. This letter was on paper and written only to me. He'd read an essay I'd written about growing up without him. His letter was short, but emotional, and after reading it twice, I felt confused. He expressed searing bitterness toward my mother and gave me what was either a blessing or a curse. I couldn't tell. After I read it, I felt like a kid who's gotten lost in the grocery store: staring up at the brightly lit shelves, passing tall strangers engrossed in shopping, certain I'll never find my way out of there. I slipped the envelope into the bottom of a drawer, hidden under hanging files in my cabinet.

In the wider world, things seemed especially violent and grim. Racism bubbled up and spilled out from hateful, shadowy depths. Natural disasters seemed to target the most vulnerable among us. There were terrifying mass shootings at schools and movie theaters and military bases. Immigrants died in their desperate attempts to flee war zones. Rapes of women on college campuses had become so prevalent that they hardly made the news. ISIS and Boko Haram stole girls from their schools, bombed places of worship, and raped and beheaded kidnapping victims. Police officers in the United States shot and killed unarmed African American men, again and again. It all seemed too awful for words. Scrolling through the news, I felt like we were all in that Ray Bradbury story and someone had gone back in time and stepped on a butterfly and now the bad guys had won. "Can't we take it back? Can't we start over?"[1]

In this season of broken appliances and loneliness and heartbreaking news stories, doubt silently pricked at my faith. I wished for more abundance, more ease, more success. I prayed for good news in my own life and in this sad old world of ours. But the bad news kept coming. I wanted Father God or Mother God or Christ my brother to show me that I was loved, that we were loved, that everything was going to be all right. (Remember in *Talladega Nights* when Will Ferrell's character, Ricky Bobby, thinks he's on fire and runs around the racetrack in his underwear? "Help me, Jesus! Help me, Jewish God! Help me, Allah! Help me, Tom Cruise!") Under a calm exterior, I was Ricky Bobby. Anxious, running in circles, ridiculous, frantic. And God's answer? Only silence.

One of my daughters bought me a plaque for Mother's Day. With an excerpt from Jeremiah 17:7, it read: "Blessed are those who trust in the Lord." She's not much of a "Christian plaque" person. Nor am I, but this moved me. Was it a gentle message from the Divine? To hold on a bit longer? To trust? As an American, I've been groomed into believing that affluence and well-being (#blessed!) are signs of God's presence and favor, and when they are absent (when we are weak or ill, when our finances are strained, or when we feel fear or doubt), God is not near. Or, put another way, God is a sort of Santa Claus, and we can tell whether God is with us by how full our stockings are.

After the publication of her book, *Blessed: A History of the American Prosperity Gospel*, historian Kate Bowler was forced to accept much more challenging news than the demise of a dishwasher or her laptop or crushing current events a world away. She learned that she was critically ill with stage IV cancer. She was thirty-five years old, a person of faith, and the married mother of a toddler. (#blessed, indeed.) While writing *Blessed*, which was widely praised for its thorough and even-handed examination of the roots and current-day iterations of the prosperity gospel, Bowler saw a common thread among its adherents. She learned that they needed to be in control.

"The prosperity gospel has taken a religion based on the contemplation of a dying man and stripped it of its call to surrender all," Bowler writes in an essay. "Perhaps worse, it has replaced Christian faith with the most painful forms of certainty. The movement has perfected a rarefied form of America's addiction to self-rule, which denies much of our humanity: our fragile bodies, our finitude, our need to stare down our deaths (at least once in a while) and be filled with dread and wonder. At some point, we must say to ourselves, *I'm going to need to let go*."[2]

I realized I was stuck in a rut that I'd carved myself. I dug deeper in prayer and confessed my greedy, wrongheaded spirituality. I confessed being an American (*For what it's worth, God, as you know I didn't actually* choose *to be born here*) and letting my country's values (or lack thereof) seep into me, replacing gratitude with greed, love with envy. I confessed that I'd been trying to force God into my own image of what God should be like.

"My idea of God is not a divine idea," C. S. Lewis admitted. "It has to be shattered time after time. He shatters it Himself. He is the great iconoclast. Could we not almost say that this shattering is one of the marks of His presence? The Incarnation is the supreme example; it leaves all previous ideas of the Messiah in ruins."[3]

That Great Iconoclast kept crushing the image I made of the Creator. Somewhere, deep within me, I knew this was important spiritual work, but at that moment, I'd rather have had my prayers answered in a more benign way. It would be a few years before I could see that God was working in me all the while, working quietly in the dark.

And then, on top of it all in this lonely, "Please send chocolate" kind of year, when I was drowning in deadlines and self-pity, I had been called to jury duty. Jury duty. Two little words that evoke such eye rolling and labored sighs. But little did I know that this responsibility would help me to, as Frederick Buechner writes in *Telling Secrets*, "unclench the fists"[4] of my spirit, shake off that sinister cloak I'd wrapped myself in, and let the light wash over me.

I'd already postponed jury duty twice over the past few months, once for a speaking engagement and a second time because I was going out of town for a wedding. There was no dodging it this time. Anyway, I doubt mine would have constituted a valid request for excusal, even if I could squeeze it into the three, narrowly-spaced lines of the reply form. What would I write?

Please pardon me from jury duty. I'm feeling terribly sorry for myself at the moment. Thank you very much.

My mood felt like a low-level depression, like I'd been flung back into the ache of wounds and insecurities I thought I'd resolved long ago. My feelings were getting the upper hand, no matter how hard I pushed back against them.

I arrived at the court building bright and early on my assigned day of service, obediently dressed in "business casual." Per the court's instructions, I had not brought along chemical sprays, garden tools, scissors, or guns. (What a world.) I passed through the metal detector and security and was directed into a large waiting room. I checked in, received my yellow juror's badge, and was shown the handwritten number on the reverse side.

"You're number 112," the receptionist said.

The room was too warm. People working in the kitchen of a nearby cafeteria laughed shrilly and clattered metal trays. There were TV screens scattered throughout the room and they showed home and garden programs. One featured crabby realtors and unpleasant buyers, their ugly bickering and greed poisoning the air in the jurors' lounge as though sulfur had been blown through the air vents. Again and again, the loudspeaker hummed, the woman's voice asking for our attention.

Not me. Not 112, I silently begged.

"2, 18, 44, 79, 110, 123 . . ."

The unlucky ones gathered their things and made their way to courtrooms. The rest of us breathed a sigh of relief. Spared again, but still held captive to the waiting. It was a strange, uncomfortable room to be in, a waiting place where I hoped for the best, hoped that I'd soon be relieved from the home and garden shows, the tedium, the lack of control. I glanced around at the strangers around me, seated at desks and tables, stopping to look up at the ceiling speaker when numbers were called. We didn't speak to each other but wore identical yellow badges, all of us trapped in the same situation. Waiting. Hoping. Not knowing whether this break in our usual schedules would last a day or if we'd be called to serve a case whose trial would take weeks. We were all very aware of the clock on the wall. At four o'clock, we would be released, and if our numbers hadn't been called by then, we wouldn't need to return.

I opened my book to where I'd left off the night before. "We keep praying that our illusions will fall away," Richard Rohr had written. "God erodes them from many sides, hoping they will fall. But we often remain trapped in what we call normalcy. . . . To get out of this unending cycle, we have to allow ourselves to be drawn into sacred space, into liminality. All transformation takes place here."[5]

I dozily reflected on waiting rooms and liminal spaces. Maybe this day at the courthouse was a reminder. Maybe I had been too aggressively resisting the in-between space where I'd found myself for the past several months, "Please send chocolate" mantras and all. Could this sterile waiting room in the courthouse be, somehow, a sacred place? A place where I could find transformation? What good had all my sleepless nights trying to make sense of the world afforded me? There was no figuring out why bad things happened—annoyances, tragedies, disappointments. What could it mean to be truly blessed, to trust in God, as that plaque from my daughter promised?

After hours of quiet meditation, I felt something like peace wrap itself around me. I felt a divine sense of camaraderie. As if God were sitting beside me, lightly punching me on the shoulder, affectionately poking fun of me in the jurors' lounge. *Oh, come on, Jen. You can manage this. Trust me on this.* My mood lifted, and I felt a surge of gratitude for this existential time-out, for this day of waiting. I closed my eyes, breathed out a long sigh. Then the woman's voice interrupted my thoughts. It was four o'clock, and we were free to go.

SEVEN

Contributors' Notes

On my seventh birthday, I was given Robert Louis Stevenson's *A Child's Garden of Verses*. The cover is burgundy, the title in gold lettering. My mother's message on the first page, dated 1974, is printed carefully, the way we write notes to small children so they won't have trouble deciphering them. Such a gift, I was sure at the time, was only given to someone old enough to appreciate it. Owning it gave my life consequence.

I read the poems carefully, and I fell in love with Stevenson's writing. For the poet, birds not only fluttered, but *quarreled*. (Yes, yes, yes—they *did* quarrel. I'd heard them in the willow tree out back for as long as I could remember.) Stormy nights *were* a man galloping by on a horse. *Galloping*, yes! I had fallen in love with poetry.

Years later, when I was a teenager, another poet named Robert captured my imagination. In his poems Robert Frost told stories as enthralling as any novel I'd ever read. I didn't want the story to end in "The Death of the Hired Man." I could *see* that "small sailing cloud" hit the moon. I *knew* Mary and Warren. I could hear their argument as if the two of them were in the next room, and most loved their definitions of home as where, "when you have to go there, / They have to take you in" and "Something you somehow haven't to deserve."[1] This poem, and so many more, taught me to think, to delineate my own ideas of place, of relationship, of self.

In college, my friend Jon gave me Wendell Berry's poetry collection *The Wheel.* Ever since I first read it, I've left the cover flap between pages 14 and 15 to mark "Rising." In it, the speaker, in his "awkward boyhood," follows the farmer up and down the rows. The elder works by desire while the younger works by will, after staying out all night. "He troubled me to become / what I had not thought to be," the younger man says.[2]

That phrase—like so many in the poems whose words have carved themselves into my memory—has become a part of me. I now read it through the eyes of a parent: How can I "trouble my children" to become what they've not yet thought to be? I read it through the eyes of my faith: In what ways is God "troubling" my spirit to become what I've not yet thought to be?

Over the years, I've drunk in the words of Auden, Finch, Plath, and Blake. Ever thirsty for new voices, I've splurged on literary journals after seeking them out in the out-of-the-way corners of expansive bookstore chains or in dim, dusty city bookshops, stacked near the counter. Opening a literary magazine, it's been my habit to page past short stories and essays, ever on the lookout for exquisite lines of poetry that catch me up in their melancholy or severe beauty.

But now, on rewarding myself with a new literary magazine—sort of like eating dessert first—I skip past not only the prose but also the poems. I find myself drawn to a section that I once thought dull: the contributors' notes. Now the writers' bios are what most capture my interest, even more than delicately crafted images or outpourings of love, hope, grief, or disbelief in the pages that precede them.

I read the contributors' notes to discern how other writers craft a life by way of the classes they teach, the anthologies they publish, and the ideas, faith, and doubt that linger with them. I suppose it's because, in my forties, I am starting to see the ways that my work, the friendships I've lost and gained, the jobs I've had, and the marriage and faith I tightly hold to are beginning to take shape.

The mystery of how lives and careers and bodies of work come together compels me, so I hurry straight to the back of the magazine, hungry for answers as I fit the shards of glass of my own life—the relationships, the writing, the convictions, and the memories—into a carefully constructed mosaic.

EIGHT

Holding Up a Mirror

After the performance, the cast jogged out from backstage for the curtain call. They weren't met, however, with the applause they might have expected. Instead, they faced a mostly silent, almost motionless—and dwindling—audience. The silence was awkward. You might even call it *punitive*. "Clap louder," I whispered to my daughter. "We're the only ones." We weren't actually the only ones clapping, but no one in the rows immediately around us made a sound.

I'd dreaded seeing the show that night, and yet there I was, clapping wildly. What a difference ninety minutes of debauchery can make.

I should back up. My thirteen-year-old daughter, her friend, and I stopped off in a small town en route to a camp in northern Michigan where I would deliver them the following morning. A friend gave us tickets to *Romeo + Juliet* (yes, it was +, not *and*) and the girls were eager to go. I'd read and seen the play in various forms about a dozen times, but the truth is the plight of these lovers had never once moved me. The feuding parents.

The saccharine balcony scene. The inept, herb-wielding priest. The fake death, the real deaths, and the prince's final reprimand. Cue the lute. (Gag.)

But this performance of *Romeo + Juliet* eschewed syrup for something quite spicy. It was violent and gritty, and most of the action took place in a graffiti-coated urban lot. Lords Capulet and Montague appeared to be warring drug kingpins, rich, hedonistic, and brutal. The bawdy bits in the text that are normally skimmed over or completely ignored were unrestrainedly explored. The nurse, for example, teases Juliet incessantly about sex, saying she'll soon "fall backward" and "bear the burden" at night. The actress playing the nurse made sure that we all knew precisely what she was talking about. Saucy! When, in Act 1, Romeo and his pals procured drugs from under a manhole cover and then passed around a lit pipe, several audience members walked out of the theater. More would follow when Mercutio mounted a fire hydrant and, well, let's just say, moved in a suggestive manner.

But all that was child's play compared with what took place at the Capulets' big party. Under a percussive blinking stoplight and blaring hip-hop music, the Capulets and their friends gyrated as if they were cast in a Lady Gaga video. Their costumes were adorned with whips, chains, leather, zippered face masks, and leashes. Romeo and Juliet were the only young people dressed in clothing that pointed neither toward inflicting or receiving pain for pleasure.

Back at the hotel that night, I called my husband to check in and tell him about the show. Eager not to introduce an unfamiliar concept to the girls, who were watching TV nearby, I searched for a way to describe the costumes in the party scene.

"There was a lot of leather," I said. "And, um, dog collars."

To my daughter, it was simpler. "Dad, it was so weird," she called toward the phone. "They all dressed up like Nazis."

Yeah, that's it: *Nazis*.

But at the heart of this raunchy, noisy show were Shakespeare's words, and somehow despite it all—or maybe *because* of how jarring it was—I was able to hear them for the very first time. I'd never before realized how much *Romeo and Juliet* simmers with hate and violence. I guess I was always too focused on the young lovers' impending doom. Now I saw how the venomous hatred shared by the elder Capulets and Montagues echoed through the story, had infected their hearts and community, and would poison their children to death.

Although I'd heard or read it so many times before, Lord Capulet's stunning cruelty to his daughter Juliet, when he realizes she will not obey him and marry his friend Paris, shocked me. He switches from being an ostensibly loving, generous father to an abusive one. "Hang thee, young baggage! Disobedient wretch!" he hisses. After striking her, he tells his cowering daughter that if she doesn't obey him and marry Paris, he will disown her and let her "hang, beg, starve, die in the streets":

> But, as you will not wed, I'll pardon you:
> Graze where you will you shall not house with me:
> Look to 't, think on 't, I do not use to jest.
> Thursday is near; lay hand on heart, advise:
> An you be mine, I'll give you to my friend;
> And you be not, hang, beg, starve, die in the streets,
> For, by my soul, I'll ne'er acknowledge thee,
> Nor what is mine shall never do thee good:
> Trust to 't, bethink you; I'll not be forsworn.[1]

That Juliet's father, Lord Capulet, in *Romeo + Juliet*, received cases full of cash and cocaine from his friend Paris in return for Juliet revealed the ugliness of this transaction in a fresh way.

Not surprisingly, my young companions for the evening were more interested in the love story. "Romeo was so hot," I heard them giggle as we went to bed that night.

I'll admit it: I cried for those star-crossed lovers as they lay on their deathbed. My daughter and her friend cried too. "I couldn't believe that they died!" the friend had said, sniffling, as we walked out of the theater. "In *Gnomio and Juliet*, they live happily ever after." (*Gnomio and Juliet*, I then learned, is an animated kids' movie based very loosely on the Bard's original text and featuring—you guessed it—garden gnomes.)

When I asked the girls if they found the play inappropriate, they just laughed. "Have you seen Miley Cyrus's new video?" my daughter asked.

So after ninety minutes of coarseness and true love, kindness and cruelty, greed and sacrifice, I was left disturbed—not by Juliet's almost see-through nightgown or Mercutio's drug pipe, but by the biblical concept that has most haunted me: the idea that the sins of the parents will be visited on the children and the children's children (Exodus 34:6-7).

On the long drive home the next day after I dropped the girls off at camp, I thought about Lord Capulet. In what ways is my love for my children conditional, self-serving, and vacillating like his? What sins am *I* at risk of passing down? How can I heed the call of the prince at the start and end of *Romeo and Juliet* and make peace with my soul and throw my "mistemper'd weapons to the ground"?[2] How can I stay awake, year after year, to all that is venomous in my own heart—my own prejudice, hatred, and whatever is most needy and desperate—so that I won't pass these poisonous things down to my children?

In an interview with Bill Moyers recorded in *The Power of Myth*, Joseph Campbell says, "Shakespeare said that art is a mirror held up to nature. And that's what it is. The nature is your nature, and all of these wonderful poetic images of mythology are referring to something in you. When your mind is simply trapped by the image out there so that you never make the reference to yourself, you have misread the image."[3]

Seeing *Romeo + Juliet* had done for me what good art can do: it held a mirror up to my soul, gave me a glimpse of my shadow self, and reminded me of my own tendency for self-justification. I was grateful for the shock of it.

NINE

Of Teenagers and Flight Attendants

Good afternoon, ladies and gentlemen. If I could have your attention for a few minutes . . ." Predictably, the other passengers and I failed to look up when the flight attendant issued this request. Some stared down at their phones, some feigned sleep. Many of us wore earbuds, muting her voice. A man across the aisle from me fed himself fistfuls of potato chips, almost robotically. Hand into bag, fist raised to mouth, hand back into bag. Crinkle, crinkle; crunch-crunch.

"Again, ladies and gentlemen, I just need a moment of your time . . ."

I closed my eyes and let my mind wander. That the flight attendant seemed genuinely bothered that no one was paying attention made me wonder whether she was new to this line of work. What other jobs might she have held? She looked to be in her forties, like me. Maybe she was an empty nester, beginning a new career or returning to an old one.

But then, all of a sudden—perhaps due to the rising tension in her voice coupled with the fact that so many of my fellow passengers were hunched over tiny, lit-up screens—her predicament felt eerily familiar. I opened my eyes and sat up straight. *It can feel just like this sometimes*, I thought, *to be the parent of teenagers*. Not always, of course, but yes, sometimes.

There are telltale signs that your child is moving into adolescence. If a once affectionate child begins to pull away, to glower at requests that he fasten his seat belt, or to snub gentle appeals that she keep her room tidy, it is likely happening. And, as parents, we can feel slighted, even invisible. Just like that flight attendant.

It's such a stark change from when children are little and we can control so much of the stories of their lives—what they eat, when and with whom they spend their time, and even, to a large degree, how they make sense of the world.

"We don't throw sand," we say. And, usually, they stop.

"What's the magic word?" we ask. And, usually, they say please.

"No cookies until after dinner," we command. And, usually, they wait.

But things change when they hit adolescence. Our kids begin to prefer the company of their friends to time with us. They no longer follow our advice about what to wear or what books to read. Whereas they once found us endlessly funny and entertaining (Peekaboo! Silly songs in the car! Kitchen dance parties!), often they find us mildly annoying. Or worse. Most of all, they want *space*.

Some of that passes, of course, but we have to acknowledge that this is all as it should be. Since their births, we've raised them with the hope that they'll be strong adults and able to make their ways in the world, independent of us. They need to develop their own friendships, cultivate their own senses of humor, and put their own moral convictions to the test. So to accomplish all this and more, adolescents must engage in countless thorny, but crucial, tasks related to separating and in- dividuating from their parents.

Like a seasoned flight attendant, we're happier when we do not take our kids' changing moods or behavior personally but remain focused on clearly communicating directions about safety, monitoring their progress academically and socially, and connecting in authentic ways with them. (Our journeys will be much smoother, too, if we provide snacks at regular intervals.)

Humbled at my epiphany about the flight attendant, I met her gaze just as she was giving the straps of the oxygen mask a tug and instructing us to secure our own first before helping others. I nodded in acknowledgment, as though this were sage and novel advice. She smiled brightly at me.

Hours later, likely in gratitude for my attentiveness, she brought me a little bottle of chardonnay—without my asking or having to pay for it. You see, when passengers treat flight at- tendants—or teenagers treat their parents—with respect, they just might receive unsolicited perks. And regardless of delays or other inconveniences, it is good to remember that this journey will indeed come to a close, and, on the other side of it (if all has gone reasonably well), we'll walk down the jet bridge together, closer than we were before, more like peers, and ready for what this new, exotic destination holds.

Eleven things flight attendants and mothers of teens have in common:

1. We sometimes feel invisible—except when there is turbulence or a delay.
2. We spend a lot of time picking up empty chip bags and soda cans.
3. We repeat ourselves—a lot.
4. We care about seat belts.
5. We don't enjoy speaking to people who are wearing earbuds.
6. We don't recommend smoking and, in fact, forbid it.
7. We like it when laptops and other devices are stowed away, out of sight, for long periods of time.
8. We don't always see the best selves of the people we serve; nor do we always show our best selves to the people we serve.
9. We fabricate a positive attitude sometimes, but everyone can tell when we're faking.
10. We get cranky when people hover near the kitchen area.
11. We are doing our best to get people safely to their next destination.

TEN

Elton John Glasses

According to my teenage daughter, I look not only old but also weird in my new glasses. I admit that the woman at the optometrist's office *did* mention that not everyone can wear these particular frames, but she assured me that I could. And I quote: "Not everyone can pull off those frames, but you? You're rocking them!" I walked out of that office with a little spring in my step.

A few days later, unbespectacled at the time, I drive my daughter and one of her friends to Starbucks. They sit together in the back seat of the car, looking down at the screens on their phones.

"My mom has 'new glasses,'" my daughter announces, apropos of nothing. She speaks the words "new glasses" in gigantic air quotes to underscore her disdain. (I silently applaud myself for not telling her that they are bifocals.) I suspect that my daughter is bound, a certain number of times each month, to some secret pact to show scorn for my appearance, the sound of my laughter, or my (infrequent) attempts to be fashionable. Apparently she hasn't yet met her quota.

I'd recently read in a book about parenting teens that "going after Mom is a girl's bid to individuate and gain recognition as a different, competent, and unique person. Through bickering, girls can affirm that they are separate selves, and the more exaggerated the conflict, the greater the assurance that 'I'm not anything like my mom.'"

"In other words, daughters are spoiling for a fight, but they still want the connection," the authors write.[1] I know all this *intellectually*, but—too often—I can't help taking it personally.

My daughter's friend glances up from her phone screen to meet my gaze in the rearview mirror before looking away again, disappointed not to see said glasses.

"She says they look 'eighties,'" I say to the friend. I try to make the descriptor sound jaunty, try to save face. My voice hardly sounds like me. It's high, anxious. I wonder for the hundredth time—why do I let this stuff get to me?

This is age appropriate.

She is doing the hard work of separating.

This is what it's supposed to be like.

"Eighties?" my daughter's friend says. "I love the eighties!" That the friend's enthusiasm is insincere is only *barely* detectable. She is trying to be courteous, even reassuring, to my doddering self. I appreciate that.

"Yeah, but they're eighties in a *really bad way*," my daughter says.

I decide that if my new glasses are "eighties," they belong in The Smiths' video "Stop Me If You Think You've Heard This One Before," in which Morrissey and the rest of lads wore glasses and cycled around that bleak English town. "I still love you, oh, I still love you . . ."[2] I sing while eyeing my daughter in the rearview mirror.

They can't hear me over the sound of the radio.

A few years ago, I watched a few episodes of a sitcom called *I Hate My Teenage Daughter*. My own daughters were just on the cusp of adolescence at the time, so some of the issues the show explored felt foreign to me. But I thought the writers were on to something in the show's premise: that having a teenage daughter makes one's own most painful or wince-worthy memories resurface. Some days I think having teenage daughters has cured me of my vanity. On others, I believe it makes me more self-conscious, more intent on looking good, more prone to scrutinizing my appearance. I flip back and forth—totally unconcerned about my appearance one moment and then bowled over by embarrassment the next. It stung when my daughter said I looked old and weird in my new glasses. I'd been feeling self-congratulatory, even giddy about them—like a five-year-old with new sneakers.

Lisa Damour is a clinical psychologist who has worked with countless adolescent girls in her practice—and this expertise shows. In her book *Untangled*, Damour defines seven "developmental strands" in a girl's maturation. These are: parting with childhood, joining a new tribe, harnessing emotions, contending with adult authority, planning for the future, entering the romantic world, and caring for herself.

Each section of Damour's book deeply explores those transitions, clarifies what is appropriate for each stage, and offers suggestions for parents on how to handle the particular challenges that attend each of them. Damour not only understands girls but also the vulnerability parents can feel when a warm relationship with a daughter seems to turn—for a time—ice-cold. She warns readers not to take their daughters' outbursts or apparent rejection personally, but to recognize these as markers that their daughters are readying themselves for the time when they will be out of the house, on their own.

"Despite the fact that it has long been normal for teenagers to hold their parents at arm's length, most of us feel rocked by the seismic shift in our relationship with our daughter," Damour writes. "The urge to hold you at a distance is largely an unconscious one. This means that her feelings about you change for reasons she can't explain. What she knows is that you used to be pleasant company but you have become inexplicably annoying."[3]

My friend Lynne recently told me, "I have been known to inform my kids that 'I am not interested in having teenagers. You take that moody crap someplace else.'"

"I wish I could be my best self every day," she sighed. "Just for my kids."

We're only human, I tell her. We can't always be our best selves. I know I can't.

When my son Theo was five years old, he calmly informed me, "Parents are actually servants who make the rules." I did feel like a servant to my kids when they were too young to make their beds, bathe, or do a hundred other things they can now do for themselves. But often the harder moments of parenthood have felt to me more like hostage situations than servitude. Aren't all of us, to some degree, held captive by our children?

A pregnant woman who is put on bed rest may feel held hostage, or maybe she will after giving birth, when she's caring for her infant. As enchanting as their tiny starfish hands are, newborns' stunning, utter helplessness holds new parents hostage—to worry, to exhaustion, and to complete, ridiculous infatuation. The child acts as kidnapper, unwittingly in total control of these large, ambling grown-ups. Otherwise sensible and accomplished adults find themselves crawling on all fours out of a darkened nursery or pretending that a spoonful of pureed peas is an airplane on descent onto the runway of their baby's tongue. The playful smile of a five-year-old holds us, delightfully captive. Later, a twelve-year-old rolling her eyes at our attempts at humor, or fiery glances from a furious fifteen-year-old: these hold us captive too. Adding to the emotional price are our own wounds, troubled pasts, unresolved hurts, and anger toward our own parents. Our desire to connect with—to love and to be loved by—our children only raises the stakes higher . . . as do our best intentions.

What I want more than anything else is to let my children go off into the world in a healthy way—free, no invisible chains. Not held hostage by their childhoods. I don't want them wearing backpacks full of burdens that they will unload for the next five, ten, twenty-five years.

I let the girls out at Starbucks and breathe out a long, soul-clearing sigh. I hadn't realized that I'd been holding my breath.

That night I have a vivid dream. In it, I am leaving my son's college dorm after a visit. I descend the stairs to the lobby and, as I am about to leave the building, his friend Kate stops me. (In my waking hours, I had not yet met Kate, but I'd been to my son's dorm several times and had seen Kate as she presents herself on Facebook.) Kate asks me to hold on and wait a minute before I leave. With the enthusiasm of a new, eager friend, she says she just wants to get to know me better. I'm her friend's mother, after all. We sit in the center of the atrium, and she leans forward in her chair, obviously spellbound by my answers to the questions she asks, rapid-fire.

"You lived where?"

"You did what?"

"Wait—when was that?"

"And so how did you end up moving there?"

"That is so cool." She draws out the words. *Sooo cool.*

In my dream, as pleased as I am to be seen as a real human being with a life story that extends beyond birthing a son so that eighteen years later I can deposit him in college, I'm uncomfortable. I feel a rising urgency to end the conversation and leave the building before my son finds me still there, talking with his friend. I glance up to the landing of the second floor, but it's empty. If he sees me, my son will think I've orchestrated this tête-à-tête and that I'm trying to insinuate myself into his college life. But it's Kate's fault—honestly!—and I keep trying to leave.

Finally, I insist that I *must* go home. I stand and begin to button my coat, but Kate asks me to come with her—just for a minute—to see a new club that she and my son have discovered. Outside the dorm, I refuse and begin to cross the street, but Kate grabs the sleeve of my coat.

"Please, come take a look, for just a second," she says. "It's just around the corner. Really, you'll love it."

I relent, in part because of her insistence, but also because I'm flattered. She obviously sees me as an interesting person— not just some nondescript, middle-aged, suburban mother, but a person who might actually like seeing a cool new club. It's cold out, and I slip my hands into my coat pockets. Kate hooks her arm through mine, companionably. Suddenly, as it happens in dreams, it is very late at night, and we have appeared at the door of the nightclub. Kate pulls a huge red door open wide, and I walk in. There's a strobe light and loud electronica music, and the place is teeming with college students.

When we reach the center of the dance floor, Kate lets go of my arm. Actually, it's more like she pushes it away from herself. Her polite demeanor drops, and she starts laughing. I realize she's brought me there to make fun of me, to point out how old and ridiculous I am. She walks away, leaving me standing awkwardly in the center of the dance floor. I look down at my coat. The cuffs of my sleeves are threadbare. I notice my hands; they are dry, and I'm in desperate need of a manicure. My veins protrude, blue and swollen.

"Like the place?" Kate calls out to me, her voice taunting. She does a disco dance move—very John Travolta in *Saturday Night Fever*—and shouts, "Love it, right?" Everyone in earshot turns, looks at me, and begins to laugh.

I spin, disoriented, desperate to find the front door, which has somehow disappeared. I follow a sign—written in some script that's foreign to me, like an odd permutation of Arabic and Swedish—that seems to point the way to the ladies' room. I glance over my shoulder and see my son, dancing. I duck and round a corner, hoping he hasn't seen me.

Finally, I find what looks to be the restroom, and I rush in. Panting, I put my hands down on the black granite counter and bow my head. Dripping sweat, I let out a deep sigh. But when I stand up straight and see my reflection in the mirror, I am shocked to find that I'm wearing glasses more flamboyant and glitzy than anything Elton John ever wore in concert, even with his most outrageous costumes. They have round white frames, and they're festooned with tall peacock feathers and gaudy sequins.

"Oh," I say aloud. "These really are eighties in a bad way."

And then, thank God, I wake up.

I fumble around in the darkness until I find my glasses, neatly folded and lying innocuously beside me on the nightstand.

ELEVEN

Two Truths and a Lie: Parents of Teens Edition

About a week before my eldest went to college, my family and I went out for Sunday lunch with his grandparents. That day, my mother and my in-laws were dealing with their own feelings of loss. They knew, after being very present supporters for the first eighteen years of his life—living only a few minutes away, sharing family dinners, sitting with us in church, and attending soccer games, school concerts, and recitals—things with their grandson were about to change. Big time. A child going off to college is not only emotionally charged for children and their parents but can also be painful for extended networks of family and friends as well.

At that lunch, one of his grandmothers asked me if I wished I could turn back time. My eldest sat beside me, his back straight, looking down at his plate. "Don't you wish he were little again? Sitting in a patch of sunshine in the yard, playing with his Legos?"

The other asked the same question, posing it differently. "Remember the sweetness of those early years? Wouldn't it be wonderful to go back?"

Their words wrung the nostalgia right out of me. No, I said. I didn't want to go back in time. I loved being an at-home mother while my kids were very small. I was all in back then, pouring myself into being the very best mother I could be. But now, I said, I was eager to see what was ahead for him. Of course, I was trying to signal something to my son while answering their questions. I wanted him to know it was all right with me that he was growing up and moving on.

Still, I felt like I was breaking a classic, unwritten rule of having a high school senior. Parents are supposed to be sentimental and even fraught—full of regret and given to ponderous rumination—about their sons or daughters growing up. But that's not what I wanted to feel or, actually, what I *was* feeling. I *didn't* want to go back in time, much as I did cherish the early years of raising my children. I loved the finger painting and bike rides. Pushing them on the swings. Holding their hands when we crossed the street. Sitting with a huge pile of picture books, reading stories. Watching as they connected with music, with friends, with ideas. Reading my boys' college application essays and getting a sense of the distinct ways they see themselves and hints of who they would become.

But each year of parenting has brought new challenges, some of which have literally brought me to my knees. I've second-guessed myself, wondered if my husband and I were making the best choices as parents. Were we strict enough? Were we giving our children enough room to grow and make their own mistakes? Were we burdening them with expectations that were too high? Did they know, beyond a shadow of a doubt, how much we loved them?

"Parenthood offers many lessons in patience and sacrifice," columnist Michael Gerson writes in a beautiful piece about his son's departure for college. "But ultimately, it is a lesson in humility. The very best thing about your life is a short stage in someone else's story."[1]

When I first read Gerson's words—"the very best thing about your life is a short stage in someone else's story"—I felt a dart to the heart. But, reflecting on them a little longer, I couldn't agree with him that the years I devoted to raising my kids would prove to be the "very best thing" about my life. I don't want that to be true—and I didn't want to put that kind of burden on my children. I don't want to keep looking in the rearview mirror, back at the intensive time of raising kids, thinking, "Those were the days," much as I will always regard those years as a precious gift. But I still have work to do, places to visit, friends to meet, and history to write with my husband. The writer of Ecclesiastes says, "Don't long for 'the good old days.' This is not wise" (Ecclesiastes 7:10), and the apostle Paul echoes that when he recommends forgetting the past and looking forward to what is ahead (see Philippians 3:13).

I also find it hard to accept that raising my kids will go down in my own personal history as the "very best" part of my life—thousands of moments were the among the best moments of my life, maybe even tens of thousands. But perhaps, particularly as I'm currently the mother of adolescents, I don't want to make such a claim. It's been a *relief*, thus far, to see my older kids walk across the stage at their high school graduations. They're in one piece, having managed to get through high school healthy and safe. It's a joy to see them bloom and mature into their adult selves. But the journey to that moment—for parents as well as for our children—isn't easy.

One night, discouraged and worried about one of my kids, I tell my husband I've been praying for our child, but I feel like there is no divine understanding of what it's like to raise adolescents. "Jesus didn't have teenagers," I say. "Lucky Jesus."

An acquaintance tweets: "Being an aware parent is a lot of work. It's not easy being responsible for other humans. To do it right it's a min 20 year full commitment." I don't know her well enough to ask her what's going on, but as she is the mother of teenagers, I can imagine ten different scenarios. Sending that tweet was her way of asking, "Can I get an amen?" I favorite the tweet and reply, "True."

If you'd told my friends and me—say, when our kids were preschoolers or in the shiny-faced days of early elementary school—that ten years later we'd find ourselves in some of the agonizing scenes that have played out since then, we'd never have believed it. Some of us have bought home testing kits for alcohol and drugs. Or learned that our child was "cutting." Parents I know have found marijuana stashed in a child's closet or tucked in with stuffed animals. We've overheard our kids using language that makes us want to wash our ears out with bleach, had to talk frankly to them about STIs, and many of us have had to just stand back and watch when they go through phases in which they recoil from us, violently, as though we had Zika virus.

Had a time-traveler visited me from the future and told me these stories, I'd have shaken my head and laughed, handed my child a sippy cup filled with watered-down apple juice, and distracted myself by singing a song from the Wiggles ("Fruit salad!

Yummy yummy!"). It was mind-blowing enough just to think about my children learning to brush their teeth on their own, let alone taking a driver's test someday. But living through those kinds of challenges? Impossible. Yet somehow we parents rise to the occasion, and we get through them. And, happily, our children almost always come out on the other side of adolescence in one piece and open their hearts to us again. But would I want to go back in time and do it all again? Um, no thank you.

I have friends who say that being *grandparents* has been the best part of their lives; this makes more sense to me. I expect when I'm older I'll be a better judge of what have and haven't been the very best times of my life—I hope to have more perspective later in life. One of my pastors, for instance, sends a reminder about an upcoming newsletter deadline. "I start the wonderful invasion of the grandblessings in a week, so would be ever so grateful to have articles early!" she writes. This woman radiates joy—whether or not she is talking about her grandchildren. I wouldn't be surprised if she considers *this* the "best time" in her life.

When my firstborn went to college, there were days when my heart felt slapped around and bruised by loss. I missed seeing his face, hearing his laugh. Making dinner every evening, I missed having him in the next room practicing his cello. I continued to set the table for six people for weeks before I got into the habit of setting it for five. But I felt something else growing in me too. It was a sense of accomplishment. I'd managed to give birth to a child, raise him, and send him off into the world to do good—and I think I was even able to achieve it without saddling him with a lot of emotional baggage. I truly liked—and like—him, enjoyed the friends he was making, appreciated the classes he chose. He was ready to go; it was time. For everything, there is a season.

And I noticed that having three kids at home, rather than four, changed our home dynamic in some interesting ways. I was able to give the younger children more attention. For those of us with more than one child, I think it's a rarely acknowledged—and guilty—secret that the first child often gets about 80 percent of the parents' attention. Every first for the eldest child is also a first for the parents. It's with that first child that we figure out how to be a parent, learn to navigate each new developmental phase, and decide what kind of home life we'd like to cultivate. By the time the next child enters school, learns to ride a bike, begins to rebel, brings home a boyfriend or girlfriend, applies to college—or does pretty much anything for the first time—parents have at least a vague sense of what their role will be and how everything might turn out. The memory has already been made, the strategy for handling it is ready to be dusted off and put to use again.

When my first left home, I realized that my time as a full-time parent really would come grinding to a stop. I had more patience for the younger ones when they needed help with homework or wanted to give me the play-by-play of a movie they saw or when they got mired in some kind of conflict. I knew to my bones, for the very first time, how fleeting it all is. Sometimes that's bittersweet; sometimes it's empowering. It is, as they say, "both/and."

On his eighteenth birthday, I asked one of my sons what he thought the next eighteen years might hold for him. Who would he be at thirty-six? What would he remember of his child-hood? He said he thought he was "about to become"—about to become the person he was always meant to be. He was about to meet the people who would most shape the rest of his life. In this moment, in the summer before college, he said he felt on the verge of starting his "real" life. I nodded and listened but privately thought that he—more than he knew—was already very much himself. He was already true to himself. He already had at least one or two true friends who would see him through the rest of his life.

I might have been wrong. Maybe my kids will surprise me over the next few years with shockingly new interests. Maybe parts of their personalities that I've not noticed or recognized will come into clear focus. Maybe they will seem very different from the people I knew as little children. I don't know. My job, at the moment, was to let him go. Let him take over the reins of his life. Sit back and watch him become an adult . . . and not spend too much time ruminating over the lost days of Lego and popsicles.

When my children were very young, I was able to fool myself into believing that I could control or completely protect them. I orchestrated so many aspects of their lives—insisting that they take their vitamins, prompting good manners, monitoring their grades, and listening to daily reports about the minutiae of their lives. But there came a moment—at the edge of their own transitions into adulthood—when I relinquished the notion that I was in control. When I faced the fact that my sometimes white-knuckled parenting wasn't, ultimately, what kept them safe or made them into the young people they are. I realized their lives have been in God's hands all along. As they ever will be.

TWELVE

Death Flickering Like a Pilot Light

I was honored to call the poet Brett Foster a friend. One of my favorites of his poems ends with the words "death always flickers in us like a pilot light."[1] It's in midlife when we find ourselves crouching down on the cold cement floor and leaning in to take a look at that quivering flame, no longer assuming that the furnace will just keep burning. When people we care about die, of course, the matter is underscored.

Brett died last year, even though I was certain that, by some wild miracle, he'd recover. He *had* to. Sure, he was diagnosed with stage IV colon cancer. Sure, he and his family somehow weathered almost a year and a half of surgeries, setbacks, and glimmers of hope. Sure, we saw his hair go silver, his body grow very thin. Still, I think everyone who knew him thought it somehow impossible that he would actually die. Somehow his genius as a poet and as a person, and the fact that he had a family to whom he was fiercely devoted and who adored him, would safeguard him from dying at age forty-two. He just couldn't go; it wasn't right. But, sadly, the cancer would not be deterred from its cruel and insistent purpose.

The last time we met, Brett took minuscule sips of his chai tea; he said he was trying to take in a few calories. After more than an hour, the drink was barely touched. As we sat at the window of the tea shop, it occurred to me that anyone who passed by us would be justified in assuming I was his middle-aged daughter or a maybe a prospective home health aide—not his friend and certainly not a person six years older than he was.

I was upbeat that afternoon, as if my own cheer could somehow loosen the grip death had on him. He was patient with me, politely suggesting that he might not be able to attend that conference, that next dinner party with our spouses, that upcoming bookstore event we'd been talking about for months. I told him what I was writing, and—as was his custom—he was curious, interested, and prompted me to deeper engagement with my work. Despite the nausea, despite the exhaustion, despite that cancer, there was something mighty about him, even in that ravaged state.

And then, not two weeks later, he died.

At the end of my street is a large park. When I walk there with my old dog Shiloh, I often use the time to pray for the people I love—and for the people I find difficult to love. I've assigned each person a spot in the park—various trees, mostly—that serve as prompts.

The prayer walk is a spiritual practice I learned from an old professor. Jim Young, or "Jimma" to his students, was the chair of the theater department at my alma mater, and on his daily walk to and from the college, he prayed for the people he loved. I imagine we numbered in the hundreds, if not thousands. Jimma had a remarkable memory for names and faces, as well as the even more extraordinary gift of loving people and acknowledging them for the specific, singular people they were. When I was with Jim—as seemed to be the case for almost everyone who knew him—I felt seen and loved simply because I was, uniquely, me. One of his signature habits was to grab hold of the end of the sleeve of whomever he was speaking to and roll the cuff up and down in careful, precise movements. It was a means of connection, a quirk that those of us who knew him duplicate when we remember him together. Jimma seemed almost lit from within, and in his loving company, it was easy to believe that a loving, creative God is the source of everything in this life and truly knows and loves us.

Even after retirement, Jim and his wife June kept a large corkboard in their home with the family photos of his students and their children, updated with cards Christmas after Christmas after Christmas. Although no longer walking to school, he continued to pray for us. Every day. When he came to visit, he would remember details about his students' families—in my case, which of my children was obsessed with marine life, which one loved to sing, and who played the cello or lacrosse. Once, years after his retirement, Jimma visited us one afternoon and, within minutes, was running and screaming through the house with my four young children, racing them up and down the basement stairs, calling out wonderful battle cries as nonsensical and dazzling as lines from Lewis Carroll's poem "Jabberwocky."

"Who was that?" one of my sons asked, his faced flushed, his bangs damp with sweat, after Jimma left. "I love him."

I aspire to be so faithful and excellent a friend as was Jimma and to grow into a faith more like his, but my prayer walk isn't a daily practice. And my own faith feels less steadfast than his. Sometimes God feels as close to me as the leaves on the birch tree in my front yard, blowing in the breeze, the tree gently stretching its arms to tap on the roof outside my window. In those moments, I'm as open and trusting as Anne Shirley, who describes "feeling" prayers in the novel *Anne of Green Gables*: "Why must people kneel down to pray? If I really wanted to pray I'll tell you what I'd do. I'd go out into a great big field all alone or in the deep, deep woods and I'd look up into the sky—up—up—up—into that lovely blue sky that looks as if there was no end to its blueness. And then I'd just *feel* a prayer."[2]

Sometimes, though, when I walk down to the park, I'm distracted or I talk to a friend on the phone or I just stomp out my bad mood on the gravel path as I circle the pond. When I'm tied in knots spiritually, I wonder whether my prayers are just thoughts blowing into the breeze. At these moments, I'm no Anne Shirley. I'm Sylvia Plath, who confessed in her journals: "I talk to God, but the sky is empty."[3]

But I continue in the practice of prayer, despite my own uncertainty and in spite of my sometimes frantic, middle-of-the-night petitions when, in the clutches of insomnia, I am filled with self-doubt and irrational requests. I beg for perks ("Please send chocolate"), blessings, and good news. These are prayers that, on waking, I half hope God hasn't heard because they are so immature and selfish. They leave no room for God's mystery or otherness; they are basically letters to Santa Claus from a spoiled child. Once again I'm Ricky Bobby shrieking and running around in his underwear, thinking he's on fire. ("Help me, Tom Cruise!")

Maybe God knows when to hit "mute."

Mother Teresa gave her life to serving God and others, yet she experienced excruciating doubt and spiritual isolation. After her death, her correspondence revealed that although she had not felt God's presence for decades, she had clung stubbornly to her faith. *Come Be My Light: The Private Writings of the Saint of Calcutta* contains personal letters written by Mother Teresa—letters she had hoped would be destroyed. These detail the agonizing doubt that plagued her: "I call, I cling, I want—and there is no One to answer. . . . Where is my faith?—even deep down, right in, there is nothing but emptiness & darkness," she wrote. "If there be God,—please forgive me."[4]

When Pope Francis declared Mother Teresa to be a saint, he referred to her as the "saint of the gutters." In the homily he gave at the canonization of Mother Teresa, Pope Francis said, "She bowed down before those who were spent, left to die on the side of the road, seeing in them their God-given dignity."[5] In the Catholic tradition, right *action* carries much more weight than right *thinking* or the "right" kind of belief. Pope Francis did not scold or cast judgment on Mother Teresa's half-century struggle with doubt; instead, he commended her as a "tireless worker for mercy." Despite her uncertainty, she continued to serve the poor and to pray to the God who felt so very far away.

I've heard people of faith, including members of the clergy, define prayer as simply surrendering our wills and egos to God—or even to the universe or to "a higher power." Others insist that prayer is a meaningful way to invite and affect change in our lives and in the world. Karl Barth, Gandhi, and others maintained that prayer is the most powerful instrument of action in a broken world. When I feel unsteady about the efficacy of prayer, I remind myself of instances in the Scriptures when the prayers of the faithful changed God's mind.[6] And that when Jesus taught the disciples to pray what we call the Lord's Prayer, he was giving us words that acknowledge that God participates in our daily lives. Hearing us. Feeding us. Guiding us. Forgiving us.

Still, it's a challenge for me to reconcile what seem to be disparate truths about the nature of God—that God is unchangeable, a mystery, and completely "other than," *and* that God's mind can be changed and that God is closely involved in the particulars of our lives, counting the hairs on our heads and keeping us from stubbing our toes. So on any given day, I am either certain that God is walking alongside my dog Shiloh and me as we wind our way around the park, or I think the sky is empty and I am just talking to myself. This tug-of-war between the skeptic and the hopeful believer serves at least one important function in my spirituality—I'm reminded, over and over again, that I cannot figure God out. There is so much I'll never know or understand about God, and all the while, the Great Iconoclast, as C. S. Lewis called God, smashes my immature perceptions of the Divine. Or, as the writer of Ecclesiastes puts it, "Just as you cannot understand the path of the wind . . . so you cannot understand the activity of God" (Ecclesiastes 11:5).

On our walk to the park, Shiloh and I pass a shrub with bright red leaves called a burning bush, and I whisper the name *Michelle*, for my friend who has been ill too long and yet still must care for her young grandchildren. Passing a row of sumac shrubs grouped along the fence by the public swimming pool, I pray for my writer friends. I say their names as I pass this cluster of bushes with their velvety fruit. *Marlena. Sharon. Lesa. Karen. Rachel. Gina.* And a dozen more. A group of seven tall pines is my place marker for my friends Mark and Mary and their five daughters. I pass by, naming them one by one. *Hear me, God. Keep them in your care.* The tree for my friend Cathleen is a sturdy oak, not young and not old, but strong, and one of the last every season to lose its beautiful red leaves. I pray for her, for resiliency, for creativity, for peace. There is a row of more recently planted trees, and these prompt me to pray for my children's eventual children. That they will be rooted in faith and love. That they will stand together, like this cluster of trees, year after year, in loving relationship.

As I make the loop around the lake and approach the park's entrance again, I cross a footbridge that has a view of a busy road, just past a large marshy area. I see the back of an old house that's now a neighborhood bar. Beside it are several dead trees. They are massive and tall, but have bare trunks and broken, jagged limbs. It is on this bridge where I pray for the people I used to know and from whom, for various reasons, I have become estranged. In these prayers, I am practicing surrender. I surrender my grudges, my hurt feelings, my unforgiveness. I pray that these people will find healing and comfort and community.

Brett's tree is a massive ash with gray, rutted bark and a scar from where a limb was chopped off many years ago. My prayer, month after month during his illness, had been that the tree would be emblematic of him—that he would live a long life and grow old, despite the visible (and unseen) scars he had accumulated during his illness and treatment. When spring came and the branches budded, I prayed for new growth and life in his body. Many times, I closed my eyes and put my hands against this tree before walking on, praying that somehow Brett would be spared, praying that God would give his wife and children courage and strength, praying that somehow every cancer cell would be obliterated from his body. Miracles do happen from time to time; I believe that. And I think everyone who knew him would have cashed in all our chips for this particular miracle to be accomplished.

Yet there I was with hundreds of others, standing graveside on a November afternoon, staring at the box that held his body. The priest dismissed us, but no one moved. No one wanted to believe, despite the weight of the evidence that confirmed it, that Brett was really gone. We stood in silence, frozen, not wanting to leave him behind at the cemetery. I've never been in close communion with such a large group of strangers. Breathing in, breathing out. In unison. After about ten minutes of stunned silence, we began to move.

Standing there, more words from Ecclesiastes rose up in my mind:

> I have observed something else. . . . The fastest runner doesn't always win the race, and the strongest warrior doesn't always win the battle. The wise sometimes go hungry, and the skillful are not necessarily wealthy. And those who are educated don't always lead successful lives. . . . People can never predict when hard times might come. Like fish in a net or birds in a trap, people are caught by sudden tragedy" (Ecclesiastes 9:11-12).

I looked up from the ground to see my friends Andy and Katy walking toward me.

"This just sucks," Andy said, opening his arms wide.

Blunt and unpoetic and honest, it was exactly the right thing to say. Crass, simple words after a day of being bathed in streams of elegant ones. Poems written by Brett's friends. Moving eulogies. Liturgy from the Book of Common Prayer. Hymns. Scripture.

Blessed are they that mourn: for they shall be comforted.

The Lord shall preserve thy going out, and thy coming in: from this time forth for evermore.

Be thou my vision, O Lord of my heart; naught be all else to me, save that thou art.

The Lord is my shepherd: therefore can I lack nothing.

The beautiful words, and many more, were meant to give our battered hearts comfort—and they did. They were meant to honor and acknowledge the life that Brett led—and they did. They were meant to point our attention toward eternal things—and they did. But I liked Andy's short poem too. Because, when we realize that death is flickering inside us, when parents and friends and others we love die, we hold our hopes in the same hands as we hold our grief.

And Brett's death, as happens whenever someone we love dies, brought the pain of other griefs to the emotional surface, and I found myself aching again for earlier losses.

THIRTEEN

What Is Left of Her

White cardboard, a little larger than a brick, the box sits high on a shelf at the back of my garage, tucked between a bin of Christmas lights and a stack of folded tarps. On the shelves below it are fishing poles, terra-cotta flowerpots, and crates full of beach toys and in-line skates. You might think the box holds a replacement part, a new spray nozzle, or some other piece of hardware. Or maybe a wind chime, sleeved in plastic, not yet untangled and hung. Its contents, however, are not the usual stuff of garages or garden sheds.

The box contains my sister. Rather, it holds what is left of her.

A few years ago, at lunch with one of my priests, I asked whether a person needed a permit from the park district or the county to scatter ashes. "Well," she said, readying her next bite of pad thai, "it sort of depends. But generally there's a 'don't ask, don't tell' policy on such things."

At the time, I thought Susan would make only a short stay in my garage. She'd sat on the shelf in the garage of one of my brothers for a few years before coming over to mine. When I brought her home, it was to release my brother and sister-in-law from the burden of walking past the box every day and wondering what to do with her. Our conversation about her presence in their garage might have sounded to a stranger as if we were discussing a houseguest who'd overstayed her welcome.

"I can take her," I said.

I had planned to scatter her remains somewhere beautiful. Maybe I'd invite my brothers on a walk in the woods to release her, or perhaps we could drive downtown to a beach in Chicago and let her remains disappear into the water at Lake Michigan. Once, in a daydream, I pictured making a trip to the Scottish Highlands with her ashes and returning her to the soil where so many of our ancestors had lived and died. I've been to Scotland since her death, but I did not take that box with me. Maybe I'm holding out for just the right way to take care of her remains. Or maybe, after many years of not knowing where she was, something in me isn't ready to let her go.

"I know why she's still there," my husband told me a few nights ago. "Because, you know, nobody ever knew what to do with her."

It was mild a few years ago in December, unusual for northern Illinois. One Saturday, my husband went out to his vegetable garden to tear shriveled bean vines from the fence, rake up dried leaves, and pull up dead plants. He then scooped heaping mounds of ash onto the garden and spread it around. They were tasks he hadn't had time for when autumn came.

"Why is he doing that?" my younger daughter, then ten, asked, watching from the kitchen window.

I launched into a short lesson on "slash and burn agriculture," grateful for the chance to call up knowledge I'd retained from my college anthropology classes. I explained that although he didn't set fire to his garden last fall, her father was nourishing the soil with potassium and other minerals and reducing the soil's acidity by spreading the ash there. We'd reap the benefits next July and August, I told her, when we ate his green beans, zucchini, and tomatoes.

"Isn't that wonderful to think about?" I asked.

"I don't know," she murmured. "It will almost be like we are eating *her*."

"What?" I asked. "Eating *who*?"

"The ashes," she said. "Isn't that your sister?"

My daughter was, as you might imagine, much relieved to hear that these ashes came from our fireplace and were not my sister's remains. I decided against telling her that, from what I'd read, "cremains" are more like gravel or sand than smoky wood ash.

Several years ago, my friend Jon Sweeney published an essay about his parents' intention to be cremated after their deaths. They first broached the subject with Jon and his brother while on a family vacation in Italy.

"Dust to dust, that is what seems right," Jon's mother had said over dinner.

Jon found it impossible, in the moment, to articulate fully why the idea of his parents' cremation so troubled him. Several months later, after much thought, he wrote them a letter, outlining why he would rather they be buried than cremated. In it, he cited the sacredness of the human body and the traditional Christian belief that, very literally, human bodies will be resurrected at Christ's return.

"Even if we separate the soul from the body at death, your body remains the sacred vessel (not a 'prison,' as some mystics have said) for your soul here on earth," Jon wrote. "It was composed out of the earth, as we know from Genesis, and to the earth it should return. Cremation takes into our hands what the earth can easily and fruitfully accomplish on its own, in its time."[1]

Although Jon's essay and the letter to his parents contained within it are poignant and thought-provoking, I still lean toward getting cremated. If there is an ultimate "Meet-Up in the Sky" at Christ's return (a theological point I have never felt compelled to defend or reject), couldn't a body be miraculously reconstructed regardless of whether it was incinerated or had decomposed in a box in the ground? Does God need skeletons to be intact for this whole "bodily resurrection" business? What about people who are killed by bombs detonating or whose bodies are decimated in ten other ways? And doesn't it seem a better use of space to be transformed into five or six pounds of gravel and hightail it into an urn rather than take up so much land?

My own church has a lovely columbarium. I've often considered purchasing two adjacent spaces for my husband and me. I once took my friend Anthony to the columbarium, telling him I wanted him to know where to find me because I'd probably die first. He is, after all, ten years younger than me. "You'll come visit, won't you?" I asked, mimicking a manipulative (and neglected) mother.

Anthony laughed, and then he urged me to buy my spot right away, pointing to an empty niche on the top row.

"It's gotta be that one," he said. "Go big or go home."

Top row or not, I'd certainly prefer to be "laid to rest," as they say, in view of that beautiful garden than to be set onto one of my children's garage shelves next to the birdseed.

At their dinner in Italy, Jon recounts his mother saying, "But, I will be gone. You know that, of course. What was me will be departed."

Jon, along with being theologically snagged by cremation, rejects the practice because of his understanding of what it means both to be embodied and what it means to love another person. His response to his mother, something I've read many times since his essay was first published, still makes me pause when I consider purchasing that spot in the columbarium wall.

"Even if you accept that the body and the soul are completely distinct, and when the body stops functioning the soul lives on somewhere else, it is still wrong to obliterate the body of a person," Jon wrote. "Yours are the cheeks I have kissed, the hands I have held. There is a connection of some kind between our love and our bodies."[2]

Having Susan on my garage shelf year after year, much as it was a comfort to me initially, seems to confirm Jon's assessment of cremation. That my daughter could mistake ashes from the fireplace for her aunt's remains doesn't speak to the sacredness of my sister's body. It's true that her life was splintered by drug use, estranged relationships, and mental illness, but these things, in conjunction with my memories of my sister, aren't the whole story. She was, of course, much more than the sum of her weaknesses, mistakes, and mental health history. More than anything, at her best she thought of herself as special, and she longed for her life to be extraordinary—every moment! The banalities of regular, ordinary life and "adulting"—doing paperwork and loading the dishwasher and all the other tiresome tasks many of us do—seemed somehow offensive to her. She wanted to live, to wonder, to create.

That box on my garage shelf doesn't make me remember her laugh or the way she held her child after he was born. It doesn't evoke images of her beauty or her hopeful, vulnerable smile. It doesn't make me remember her playful nicknames for those she loved or how she painted over dreary walls and dingy, second-hand furniture with vibrant colors and designs. It doesn't point to her status as a beloved child of God.

I haven't mentioned Susan's ashes to my brothers for several years, and they haven't spoken of them either. We tend to avoid difficult conversations, maybe most especially about our family of origin. You could say the three of us are highly allergic to drama. Despite this ailment, we have found ourselves thrust right into it many, many times over the years—and these dramas often had something to do with our sister.

We have hurried down unfamiliar hospital corridors and stood around Susan's bed after receiving muddled, panicked calls from strangers. We've avoided the indecipherable stares of her friends and former lovers in broken-down apartment buildings as we've gathered her possessions by the armful, stuffing them into garbage bags, the trunks of our cars, or sometimes straight into Dumpsters in the parking lot. We've tried to be upbeat while talking with her, her teeth and lips stained charcoal black after her having her stomach pumped. We've pretended not to notice the wounds on her wrists or the restraints that fastened her arms to a hospital bed as she woke into consciousness. We've paid rent, hired therapists, cleaned, done mountains of laundry, and cared for her child. We were never able to turn her life around.

Sometimes, when discussing homelessness in America, someone will burst forth with self-righteousness, stating what seems (to him or her) to be obvious: "How can this even happen? Where are these people's families? Why don't they take care of their brother/sister/parent/child? Why don't they get them the help they so desperately need?"

I know from experience that it's usually not that easy.

I wish it were.

David Sedaris, in an essay called "Now We Are Five," tells the story of the long-planned family vacation that he, his surviving siblings, and their father took only a few weeks after his sister Tiffany's suicide. Before the trip, his sister Amy traveled to Tiffany's apartment to clear it out. Amy found signs of the poverty and mental illness that had plagued their sister. A dresser with missing drawers. A mattress on the floor. A strange collection of mop handles. A single paper plate. Torn family pictures. Amy gathered two boxes of her sister's personal things and packed them away. Sedaris writes:

> "Just awful," my father whispered. "A person's life reduced to one lousy box."
>
> I put my hand on his shoulder. "Actually there were two."
>
> He corrected himself. "Two lousy boxes."[3]

So much about Sedaris's sister Tiffany and her death resonate with my experience of my sister Susan. Like Amy Sedaris, I gathered "two lousy boxes" of possessions from Susan's room after she died. In my case, it was two laundry baskets and two brown paper grocery bags. There were two vintage, beaded sweaters. A long, green wool army coat. A leather skirt. A black velvet dress. There was an old cell phone, a computer mouse, and a composition book. I paged through empty pages and found a few jotted notes. The pages were wrinkled—coffee or another dark liquid stained and warped them. Pages were torn from the two notebooks, and I wondered what had been taken out. It all smelled of stale cigarette smoke. What puzzled me about this collection of things weren't the six or seven pairs of sunglasses—round like John Lennon's and most with colored lenses. It wasn't the single black high-heeled pump, the sole broken and almost bent in half. It wasn't even the spiral notebook, its last entry written in March 2009—two months before her death, when the melanoma had already spread itself throughout her body and into her brain—about her exercise regime, weight, and the vitamins and supplements she was taking.

What surprised me were the Christmas ornaments and boxed greeting cards. Most were in their original packaging, many with bright orange clearance stickers from a dollar store. They were cutesy things—cheap wooden soldiers, Santa Claus figurines, elves. The greeting cards were faux elegant, with the word NOEL in script on the front. There were bunches of plastic fruit, covered in glitter. Candles. Ornaments made to look like Valentine's conversation hearts. LOVE YOU. U ARE CUTE. KISS ME. The presence of these things was a mystery to me; I always thought of her as an artist who would never be drawn to such kitsch.

Like Tiffany, Susan had separated herself from our family. Like Tiffany, my sister was at (unpredictable) turns despondent, caustic, and very funny. Both women created what we might call "outsider art." Tiffany used found glass and other objects to make mosaics, and my sister covered canvases and used furniture with paintings.

Before my sister died, I had grown accustomed to living with a low hum of worry, always half expecting a phone call informing me that she had ended her life. Long periods of silence were punctuated by rare, bewildering phone calls. Sometimes she was paranoid, sometimes grandiose, sometimes just confused and sad. From about the time I was twenty-five until she died, I would think of her and be filled with dread. I was used to living with these fears, as someone might forget he has a limp until he passes by a shop window and notices his own lurching gait.

But unlike Sedaris's sister, mine didn't take her life. Cancer did, and sadly, she wasn't able to put up much of a fight against it. By the time she was diagnosed, melanoma had spread through her body, and she had only a few weeks to live. The cancer was in her lymph nodes. It moved in her blood. "Circulating tumor cells," they called it. She was left half blind, half deaf, and covered in inky-black patches of cancer.

After she died, we held a service for her at my church, and that ruined physical body was cremated. And now her remains sit on my garage shelf. I wonder if I keep her close by because I like knowing, after a lifetime of worry, exactly where she is.

FOURTEEN

Melanoma Posters

I am not feeling particularly glamorous at the moment. I'm perched, naked except for a thin white paper gown, on an examining table. I've been instructed that even my socks need to come off for the exam. My doctor had advised, given my sister's recent death, that I needed to go to a dermatologist for a full-body mole check. (Don't some phrases seem to be just itching to be chosen as a name for a band? Next up . . . "Full-Body Mole Check!") So, anyway, here I am.

Hanging on the walls of this room are medical posters, each one as gruesome as the next. One shows two identical cross sections of skin, fat, and muscle. One is labeled "normal" and one "melanoma." Both look like neatly cut squares of layer cake—tres leches, perhaps—or even a delicate petit four. The only difference between them is that, on the melanoma piece, it looks as though someone has jammed a big, black raisin on the top. It turns my stomach.

There is a quiet knock at the door, and the doctor and nurse enter. The doctor is an elderly man with a twinkle in his eye.

(Are dermatologists particularly happy and well adjusted? It almost seems like he is about to break out into giggles.) His nurse is a middle-aged woman in her fifties, an inch of white roots showing along the part of her brown hair, and deep vertical frown lines in her forehead. She's strict and no nonsense; he's all relaxation and smiles. You could say she's the yin to his yang.

"Why are you here?" he asks me, delighted, as though people spontaneously drop by this office all the time, as though my visit is a lovely surprise.

"One of my siblings died of cancer," I say. "Melanoma."

It's been a month since my sister's death. Focusing on the side of the nurse's face, I will myself not to cry. She's angled away from me, tapping on the keys of her laptop. I'm grateful that they can't read my mind or know my most secret fear—that this doctor is about to discover jet-black patches on my skin. That I'll die of melanoma too.

"Brother? Sister?" His smile is gone, his cheer has evolved into compassion.

"My older sister," I say. The nurse continues typing.

"How old was she?" he asks.

"Forty-eight."

"And you are?"

I'm tired. I am afraid. I'm angry that she died. I am feeling sorry for myself. I'm fretting over every sunburn I've ever had.

"Forty-two," I say.

"No one should die of melanoma," he says, his voice firm.

Thanks so much, Captain Obvious.

I flinch at the judgment in his voice. The last thing my sister needs is one more person looking down on her. It's cold in here. I am nearly naked. I know that a "full-body mole check" is an invasive examination. I just want this to be *over*. And leave poor

Susan alone. Maybe no one "should" die of melanoma. Yes, she ignored the cancer that took over her body, month by month over the last year of her life. But how does it help to reprimand her now?

As the doctor pulls latex gloves from a box on the wall, I look away and another poster catches my eye. Now I can't keep hot tears back; they sting as they run down the sides of my face. The grisly images on these walls bring too closely to mind the black patches and tumors Susan showed me when I first saw her in the oncology ward, less than two months ago.

She had seen them for months, felt the bump under her arm growing into the size of a softball. She began having trouble seeing out of one eye and hearing from one ear. But she didn't seek medical care until the end. She was in denial, her brain addled by substance abuse. Unemployed, uninsured, and homeless, she was staying with a friend only about forty minutes from my home. I hadn't known where she was living for years. Or even *whether* she was living.

The doctor's cold, gloved hands spread my toes apart, gently lift my breasts, separate my hair into sections, checking my scalp. It feels like a violation somehow, as professional as he is and under the humorless, watchful gaze of his nurse. I understand her presence here, standing beside him. She's meant to be a comfort, a protection, for me.

"Now we need to check your back," the doctor says.

I awkwardly sit up and, pulling the gown around me, turn over to lie on my stomach.

I first read the Canadian novelist Robertson Davies when I was in college. Had I been a better student, I would have spent more time in the library, but instead I often found myself lost in novels, including his. Sitting on a bench or lying on the grass while my more disciplined peers scurried to class, I was captivated by Davies's trilogies. I felt sorry for the other students, scuttling off to the rat race when they could be swept away to Toronto or rural Ontario with Davies's gorgeous prose. Yes, thanks to these novels, I may or may not have missed part of my German final (among other things), but I easily forgave myself. If anything, these were literary misdemeanors, and—let's be honest—I had no intention of ever mastering German.

In my favorite of his novels, *What's Bred in the Bone*, Davies describes the influences of two supernatural beings, a daimon and an angel, who oversee the life of protagonist Francis Cornish. The daimon isn't a demon or evil force but a creative spirit who helps Cornish develop into a great artist by giving him trials—sickness, neglect, and disappointment—to overcome. The daimon criticizes his angel counterpart for being overly sentimental; he knows that Cornish will grow and deepen as a person and artist as the result of *suffering*, not by receiving fluffy blessings or having his wishes granted.

"I had a rough idea of the direction in which I was going to push him, and I always like to begin tempering my steel early," says Daimon Maimas. "A happy childhood has spoiled many a promised life. And it wasn't all unhappy."[1]

Over the years, I've built on Davies's notion of the daimon in my imagination. I've wondered if my own personal daimon is a mischief-maker who sends not only obstacles but also disruptions. In times of grief, I've almost come to expect odd, sudden distractions to arrive at the most inopportune moments. I'll be in the middle of trying to resolve a problem with one of my children, or recovering from an illness, or planning a funeral service . . . and then water droplets form and fall from the ceiling. A stray dog shows up in my front yard, barking wildly and refusing to leave. Or I'll hear raccoons scratching around in the attic. Next thing I know, I'm mopping the kitchen floor, or chasing the dog around a tree and trying to grab its collar, or calling the wildlife center, when I suddenly think: "Wait! *Daimon*? Is this you?"

And often, I can see their silver linings not long after receiving these diversions. If nothing else, they pull me away from the more difficult problem at hand, usually get me out of the house, and yank me away from grim thoughts. They give me something straightforward to *resolve*. In the end, they are helpful—unwelcome and unlikely, but helpful all the same. When I return to whatever is the more serious matter, I see it from a new perspective. I've gotten distance, and I'm more ready to tackle it. I wish I could talk to Davies about the idea of daimon as mischief-maker, but unfortunately he is no longer living. Depending on what heaven is like, perhaps I'll have the chance.

When my sister died, I once again was reminded of my theory about the distracting daimons. It was a painful, disturbing time. Her cancer was visible, devastating, disfiguring. She had an adult child whom she hadn't seen in years. My children met her for the first time on her forty-eighth birthday, two days before she died. I grieved for the string of sorrows and losses that seemed to define her life, as well as for the relationship we were not able to have. I'd have to let go of the shard of hope I'd always tucked away like a treasure, the hope that someday she would be well and that we would be close. In that time of grief, I felt neither here nor there. As if life had stopped or time was suspended—or moving, if not more slowly, in a totally different direction than it had been before.

After the death of his wife, C. S. Lewis kept a journal that became what I believe to be his very best book, *A Grief Observed*. In it, Lewis writes: "There is a sort of invisible blanket between the world and me. I find it hard to take in what anyone says. Or perhaps, hard to want to take it in. It is so uninteresting."[2]

In this strange, unhappy time, some unexpected distractions foisted themselves into the picture. A woman who had been my sister's friend decades before when they were in high school, came, as they say, out of the woodwork. Let's call her Angie. Angie said *she*, not my family and me, would plan a memorial service. She would go through my sister's things. She repeatedly phoned one of my brothers and raged about how she felt our family had wronged my sister years ago. Her accusations were vague and had the empty brittleness of a long-held, festering grudge. I hadn't seen Angie since I was a child. She'd missed the past thirty years of moving Susan and her child in and out of apartments, making those disturbing hospital visits, and so on. But, suddenly, she was putting herself in charge of what was left of my sister's life. (Oh, hi . . . is it you, daimon?)

In the end, Angie disappeared as quickly as she had materialized. She stopped calling. She offered no support to my sister's child. Although she rifled through the apartment where my sister had been staying before she died, tearing pages from Susan's journals and taking some of her possessions before my brothers and I came to pack them up, the damage Angie caused was minimal. She served as a painful distraction in an excruciating time, drew us together, and gave us something else, something other than funeral plans and our sense of devastating loss, to talk about.

At breakfast recently, one of my brothers and I were talking about our sister's death. I shared my daimon theory as we remembered Angie's behavior during that time. "Don't you think she might have been sent by a daimon? Just to distract us from the deeper grief of the moment?" I asked.

My brother cocked his head, clearly not buying it. "She made a really terrible time even worse," he said.

Two weeks before she died, Susan reappeared in my life after a decade of silence. First she was in the oncology ward, then she was in hospice care, and then she died. Ten years of silence and then two weeks of emotional tsunami. *She came back to us in the end.* That's what I say about the last weeks of my sister's life. Her life was difficult. She struggled as a single mother without a college degree. She lost custody of her only child. She had no permanent place to live. She never was the artist she dreamed of being when she was young. But she returned home at the very end of her life, and my brothers and I were able to be at her bedside when she died, praying and singing her out of this world and into the next.

That particular framing of the story is a comfort. There's resolution in it, isn't there? Coming home to family. Dying in the presence of her siblings. Speaking of her hope of heaven. Can we say it's a redemptive finale? It is a good ending, and it's factually accurate, but it's also true that when she came back, she didn't know she was so near to death . . . and there was so much pain that came before.

My brother had called me one day in early May, and he doesn't often call. "Susan's in the hospital," he said. "It's not good."

This was not the first time over the years he'd called me and spoken almost those same words. I believe, in fact, that it was the third. Susan had been hospitalized when I was in my twenties, she was assaulted by an intruder who broke into her apartment. Several years later, she attempted suicide. This call was the third time I'd be summoned into a medical emergency in her life. And it was the last. There's a symmetry in that as well, and heft in the number three. It was the third time I'd drive to an unfamiliar hospital, the third time I'd make my way through the lobby to find my sister, battered and broken in a sterile, brightly lit room.

Our memories shape who we are, and Susan found it hard to remember at the end of her life. The cancer was in her brain; it had trouble *remembering*. So I tell her story only from my own perspective. Maybe she had been in sterile, brightly lit hospital rooms many, many other times over the years. Another overdose? An abortion? Elective surgery for foot pain or a cyst? I will never know.

My sister struggled with substance abuse, I say.

She suffered from mental illness, I say.

These explanations help to explain how things went so terribly wrong for her. And they put people at ease. If it's drugs or the crazy that made her life so miserable, people can breathe deep sighs of relief. There is some sense of control, some condolence that it won't happen to them or to the people they love. Her fate won't be theirs. We can tell or hear her sad story and not feel crippled by the fear that we'll end up like her: homeless, alone, dead from a disease that—as the dermatologist said—no one should die of.

The first few times I saw her in the oncology ward, I was reminded of how much I enjoyed being with her. She joked about the perks of being there with terminal cancer. There were no dietary restrictions or visiting hours. "And free morphine!" she laughed, as though we were both there just for the drugs. One night as I was leaving, she called me back into the hospital room. "Jenni—get in here and tell me you love the 'no rule' policy on this floor as much as I do," she said, laughing. "Oncology is the place to be, right? Rock on!"

Susan was lucid only about thirty percent of the time at that point. Otherwise, she slept or, when awake, talked jovially about what she was going to do when she got out of there. How, after surgery, she was going to have a huge party with all her friends. How she would need a place to stay when she got better. How she needed to find a new job after she recovered. What she was going to do with her hair once it all came back in.

With the cancer in her brain and flowing through her blood, I wondered how any of it could be true, but hoped that—since my last visit—there was some good news. Some chance that they'd be able to treat her cancer, some chance that she might survive. "Yeah, it's going to be great when I'm better again," she said one evening. For corroboration, I glanced over at the nurse who was hovering in the corner of the room. She met my gaze and shook her head. A subtle side-to-side motion; her lips in a straight line. There was no hope.

A few days later, Susan moved from the hospital into hospice care at one of my brothers' houses. The next day, on her birthday, I had a hunch that her time was extremely short. My kids had never met her, and I wanted them to see their aunt before she died. On the way, we stopped by the drugstore and bought a birthday card, a teddy bear, and chocolate. Mia, my youngest, was just seven at the time. While I was choosing a birthday card, she walked up to me, her arms wrapped around a big blue playground ball. "Let's get your sister this for her birthday," she said. I wonder whether Martha Stewart ever addressed the issue of what are appropriate gifts for someone on his or her deathbed.

"No, no," I said. "I don't think we can take this there." Susan was lying prone by this time, struggling to stay awake, her bre●'hing labored. My daughter gave me the side-eye and trudged over to return the ball to its bin.

Walking into my brother's house with my husband and kids that day echoed of the end of *The Wizard of Oz*, when Dorothy finally returns to Kansas after visiting Oz, and her family and the farmhands surround her bed. Instead of the Tin Man, Cowardly Lion, and Scarecrow, however, it was my four young children with our teddy bear and chocolate . . . and my sister with a morphine drip and ever higher doses of antianxiety meds as her restlessness and fear increased.

We walked into the room, and on seeing my older daughter, Isabel—whom my brothers say looks "eerily" like I did as a child—my sister spoke excitedly. "You're my baby sister! You're my Jenni!"

"I want a picture of you," she said, pointing at Isabel. "I want to put a picture of you here, right next to my bed." My nine-year-old smiled, enjoying the attention.

On seeing my sons, Susan laughed that one looked like our brother Drew and the other like my husband. (Both true.) And then, on seeing my youngest, Mia, who is Latina, Guatemala-born, and whom we'd adopted in the time since I'd last had contact with Susan, my sister reached out, took her hand, and drew her close.

"I don't know who you are or where you came from," she spoke slowly, her voice overflowing with affection. "But you are *beautiful.*" Mia smiled, and she handed her aunt the teddy bear we'd bought.

Susan went in and out of sleep, occasionally telling Isabel that she was her big sister, and then saying how much she looked forward to the beauty of heaven. By the end of the day on her birthday, her breathing was more labored and she no longer woke up. She breathed hard, panting and straining to breathe, like a person running a marathon. It looked like exceptionally hard work.

Over the next two days, Susan's body failed. She slept most of the time. Her hair fell out in big chunks. She was put on oxygen. Once, in those last hours, she raised her head and looked me straight in the eyes. I was glad I was there beside her at that moment, my hand on her knee. The hospice nurse would wet a washcloth and gently wash my sister's face. She brushed her hair, clearing away what had fallen out. She made a tiny bun of what hair was left on Susan's head. My sister suddenly looked about ninety years old.

Susan died two days after her birthday. I was by her side with one of my brothers and my sister-in-law. We told her how much we loved her and told her it was okay to go. We said Jesus waited for her, welcoming her, and we sang. And, at long last, her labored breathing stopped. Little by little by little.

After she gave up the arduous work of hauling breath in and out of her body, my two siblings and I sat at her bedside. One of my brothers spoke what we all were thinking. It was the last time the four of us would ever be together again. The Grant kids. My sadness about losing my sister sometimes threated to sink me. But then something warm and deep would fill me. Was this strange, warm comfort the prayers of my friends, rising, as the psalmist says in Psalm 141:2, like incense to God? I felt bathed in peace, bathed in grace, certain that Susan was no longer there and that God had lovingly received her soul. Seeing her make this passage affirmed my faith and, for a time, my doubting heart was quieted. I knew to the marrow of my bones that ours is a loving, if utterly incomprehensible, God.

Ecclesiastes 7:3 says that "sadness has a refining influence on us," and I've found that to be true. My grief has arisen at odd and startling moments ever since. It's what I half expected, though, thanks to the words of a dear friend who pulled me aside after Susan's memorial service. "You know," he said, "I've never known you to process grief in real time. You've just been through a huge couple of weeks. You'll be managing it all for a while." He was right. How could I explain to others what it meant to lose a sister whom I hadn't known for years? Whom, in some ways, I never knew. How could I explain the joy of having had her meet my kids, at least that one time, or the mystery of being with her when she died?

I felt numb and overwhelmed by emotion—somehow all at once.

"I'm sorry about your sister," an acquaintance said as we squeezed past each other in the church narthex. "But you weren't really that close anyway, were you?"

"What?" I said, bumping into a choir member in his white robe. "No, I guess not."

Others felt the need to remind me that my sister smoked and that smoking probably "encouraged" the melanoma.

"Did you ever really know her?" someone else asked. Others wanted details, asking whether she used a tanning bed. (She had.) And whether she had ever been badly sunburned. (Yes.)

"You know, you're so fair skinned. You should be careful about that."

"Didn't she notice the cancer? I mean, it doesn't really sneak up on people, does it?"

I'd nod or shake my head or inch away, swearing to myself that the next time someone I knew was grieving, I'd say absolutely nothing at all. I'd be a meaningful forearm squeezer or a lingering hugger, but I never wanted to speak words like the ones that only sent me further into my grief.

How could I explain that Susan's dying also meant the death of a long-held dream that someday, somehow, she would get better? That we would round out the end of our lives in close relationship to each other. Or that, as with any siblings, we were part of the fabric of each other's childhoods, so that her death pulled a chapter from the book of my life, leaving part of my own story incomplete. Her death was the death of my dream that we'd have a happier ending, someday, together.

"Okay," the dermatologist says, "You can sit up now."

I turn and, struggling to cover as much of myself as I can in this flimsy paper robe, move into a sitting position on the examining table. He points at me and grins. "No melanoma."

The doctor and nurse leave the room, pulling the door closed behind them. I stand up from the table, my bare feet on the cold floor. Taking off the paper robe, it tears. I stand naked under the false, fluorescent lights. For now, I am released, free to gather up my clothes, free to get dressed, and free to leave the examination room.

FIFTEEN

A Clean, Untangled Grief

My son and I sit side by side in the auditorium on "accepted students" day. The stage is empty, save for a podium emblazoned with the university's seal. Behind it hang about forty banners, each lettered with one of the school's majors: English, chemistry, Chinese, sociology, statistics, and so on. My son stares straight ahead, his eyes wide open, focused.

Triumphant music begins, and current students sprint onto the stage and start tossing T-shirts and stuffed animals at the audience. The university's president jogs up the steps, stands behind the podium, and congratulates the high school seniors in attendance for surviving the brutal and selective admissions process. His tone is welcoming, celebratory.

"It's like you won the Hunger Games," I whisper. My son laughs.

My mind flashes to another day twelve years before, when I sat beside this child in an elementary school gym. The principal told us how excited he was to meet the incoming kindergartners and their parents. His tone was welcoming, celebratory. My serious little boy stared straight ahead, eyes wide open, focused.

Afterward, the two of us had gone out onto the playground and stood at the tetherball pole, chatting and hitting the ball back and forth before walking into town for lunch. He ordered grilled cheese, fries, and lemonade. His favorites.

I didn't take pictures of my son at the kindergarten orientation or in the restaurant. A dozen years ago, proud, nervous parents like me weren't armed with smartphones. But I did take mental pictures that day, because I knew it was a momentous one. I willed myself to remember it, thinking: "So it begins." I knew that when we crossed over to the other side of his school years in twelve years' time, he would go off to college and then depart into adulthood. This was one of a string of increasingly more poignant beginnings, all of which drew us to saying good-bye. I believed he'd still be very much himself when he turned eighteen and that he would always be my child, but he'd be his own person. Not mine to look after. We'd no longer share our days, and things would shift. I knew we'd somehow have to re-calibrate what it meant to be in relationship with each other . . . but it all seemed unimaginable back then.

Sometimes, lately, when all my kids are home and playing soccer in the backyard or sitting at the kitchen counter eating breakfast, or during any of a hundred other everyday moments, I take focused, mental pictures. I want to remember every detail of the four of them together. I know that a chapter is ending, dissolving, and pixelating, bit by bit by bit by bit. Over the next few years, as each one finishes high school and goes off to college, their numbers fall. Four to three to two to one. Before long, they will begin to create families of their own. Time when we all can be together will be spare. A kiss on the cheek. An email. A Christmas card. A reunion. When I post a picture of my kids these days, I sometimes use the hashtag "#sunrise/sunset." The lighthearted cliché masks my more complicated feelings of loss. The lines are, of course, from *Fiddler on the Roof*, when at their daughter's wedding the characters Tevye and Golde sing, "Sunrise, sunset . . . swiftly flow the days."

When children are young, however, days can feel anything but swift or flowing. A mother who spends the day perched on the edge of the bathtub, trying to entreat her toddler to use the toilet in that slow torture that is potty training, or who lies in bed awake, waiting up for a teenager to come home much later than expected, feels quite the opposite. We trudge through many, many, many days and nights. But then suddenly they're grown, itching to be independent, almost ready to leave home. These people who used to count on us to tie their shoes and answer all their questions and cross them safely to the other side of the street suddenly face enormous decisions—including where they'll spend their college years, whom they'll marry, where they will land in their careers and passions.

After the meeting in the university auditorium, my son and I stop for lunch in the student center. Standing beside me, taller than me now, he orders a grilled cheese sandwich and fries. He fills a glass with lemonade. All his favorites.

I take a deep breath, and I remind myself that this—this growth, this health, this imminent independence—was always

the goal and eventuality. We raise our kids to become independent, to move on. And although what I feel is actual grief, it's a
clean and untangled one.

Things are as they should be.

SIXTEEN

Lucky in Love

For several years, every Saturday morning found my husband and me pulling our kids out of bed, digging around in closets for their soccer cleats, tossing granola bars and juice boxes into our diaper bag, and rushing off to a huge park on the south side of town. We'd always remember our folding chairs—except when we wouldn't. Sometimes we knew which was our assigned field, but, as I look back on it now, we often crisscrossed through the park, the frigid morning dew drenching our shoes and feet, our anxiety mounting, until we finally saw a familiar face. With four children aged seven and under, getting anywhere those days was a herculean task, and we rarely felt prepared and were seldom on time.

Most of what I remember about my children when they were very young is bathed in a happy afterglow. I loved the new baby smell. Being witness to their firsts—first steps, first words, first friends. Laughing at the dinner table, family vacations, and every time our four children emerged from the basement wearing odd combinations pulled from the costume bin (pony pirate!

princess knight!) and insisted on performing the play they'd dreamed up just five minutes before. Sitting on the side of the tub while they splashed and chatted. Singing in the car. Their true delight in something as simple as ordering a double scoop of ice cream or seeing the pair of mallard ducks who took up residence in our flooded backyard every time there was a hard rain. Or watching from the window as they walked down the driveway, backpacks on, lunch bags swinging in their hands, on their way to school.

But those soccer games early on Saturday mornings?

Not. So. Much.

I remember my husband and I desperately trying to find the right field on cold mornings. I feel the strap of the diaper bag pressing down against my shoulder and collarbone and the camp chair digging into my aching back. And, oh, the futility of it all— all this effort was in service to an hour of watching little children jog up and down the field in a cluster, unsure of what they were meant to do . . . that is, when they weren't crouching down to find bugs in the grass or leaning against the goalpost, chatting with their teammates. Looking back, the only saving grace of attending those games was socializing with the other parents.

For years, there was one family in particular that grabbed my interest. You might say I was infatuated with them. This couple had only two children to our four. They pulled up in their shiny new SUV and walked onto the field, a cardboard tray neatly holding their lattes from Starbucks. Whereas, as soon as we finally set up our chairs on the sideline, David would pull down his baseball cap and read the newspaper or click away on his BlackBerry, the husband in *that* family served as a sort of unofficial greeter to the other families as they arrived at the field. He knew all the kids' names and seemed to have inside jokes with all the dads. He made the somewhat shlumpy moms—and

I'm pointing to myself here—feel as if we'd just walked out of a salon after getting a great haircut. All of a sudden, it was as though the extra twenty pounds I tried to hide under my over-sized sweatshirt would, for a moment, disappear into the thin morning air.

"Well . . . hello!" he called. (I might even have blushed.)

The wife and mother in this family was cheerful and poised. Her smile seemed to say that yes, she knew that life was, indeed, very, very good. The children were adorable redheads, freck-led, beautiful, and kind. Suddenly my own kids, with their un-brushed hair and the way they hissed over that last package of fruit snacks, seemed raggedy and untamed. Half the time, my older and younger kids would end up in the wrong jerseys. One would be swimming in his, the other wearing one he outgrew years ago. And, after our misadventures getting to the field, I was drained, my forehead beaded in sweat, my hair turning into a mass of frizz. It took David and me a solid five minutes, at minimum, to get past being miffed with each other after the events of each stressful morning.

"You said it was field E3."

"No, B3. I said B3."

"But this is *H!*"

"Can you keep your voice down? Please?"

Needless to say, David and I never managed to get out of the door early enough to stop for coffee on the way to the soccer game. Sitting down, I'd smile and wave at this other (better) couple, and they'd take a luxuriant sip of their lattes, extend their arms in a jaunty wave, and call out, "Hello!"

Why'd we have so many kids in the first place? Why does David have to be so cranky? Why can't I be as attractive and put together as that woman is? What do those two know about being grown-ups that, somehow, we missed?

So, as it does, time passed. Our children finally lost interest in playing soccer on Saturday mornings, and I lost touch with this particular family—until the day when one of my kids asked for a ride to go see one of theirs. Halfway out the door, my daughter stopped herself and said she needed to check to see whether her friend was at her mom's or at her dad's house that afternoon. The parents, she explained, were divorced and lived apart from each other. Later the mother would tell me that she had been very unhappy for a long, long time. Yes, even on those Saturday mornings when they arrived for soccer, seeming to spill over with unmitigated joy.

Their split affected me deeply. I remembered the mornings that I looked down the sidelines at them, wishing David were friendlier and I were prettier and that we were more like them. I wished we had a nicer car—like theirs. A nicer house—like theirs. Or just had any modicum of an idea of how to raise kids—like they did. I wasted time at those soccer games wondering how that family had somehow gotten everything so right, when I felt like I was just making it all up as I went along.

The irony is that, while I was enjoying a happy marriage and family life during that time, despite the occasional snarkiness and squabble, I was making myself unhappy when I compared my life to what I *thought* was theirs. As Teddy Roosevelt reportedly said, comparison is the thief of joy,[1] and after that golden couple split up, I never again felt tempted to compare my own marriage to someone else's. Now I'm quite certain that I cannot know what's going on inside a marriage—unless I am one of the two people in it. And this has made me much more grateful for the life I actually have.

And, truthfully, I've been lucky in love.

I would be a liar if I said that marrying David a few weeks after my twenty-first birthday, after dating for less than a year, was a blueprint for wedded bliss. Had I been older, I may have taken a moment to process the grave look on the pastor's face in premarital counseling when, after we took the requisite personality tests, he asked David and me to schedule an additional session. He said we needed to talk. While he didn't *exactly* encourage us to reconsider our getting married, he warned that it would be a "challenge" for us to build a life together, given how different we were. We knew we were different, but opposites attract, right? And we were very, very much in love.

"I've never seen an engaged couple with outcomes like this," the pastor said, holding up two hand-drawn graphs. Stacked on top of each other and held up to the light, they could have created an image of a broken mirror; David zigged where I zagged.

We, however, were unconcerned.

I was sure we were meant to be. After all, my fiancé had passed the *Harold and Maude* assessment. I'd decided a year or so before I met him that I'd never marry a man who didn't love that movie. On one of our first dates, I pushed the tape into the VHS and, although he was unaware that it was a test, David laughed and cried all the way through it. This might sound like a rather flighty way to determine lifelong compatibility, but thirty years later, here we are. Love is a mystery; there is no predicting who will and who won't make it for the long haul. But I'm grateful that we are still together.

Maybe our personalities and temperaments are actually like a broken mirror. We come together in an uneven, jagged pattern. When I dip too low, he fills in the gap. And I hope I do the same for him. We both have to die to self and to smash the image of who we think we are or who we pretend to be, year after year after year, in order to create a complete picture. And it hasn't always been easy.

Very early on, he admitted that he'd been infatuated with someone else for a short time after we met, and that confession surprised me and infected me with an insecurity that I couldn't shake for years. Our emotional needs—for communication and for time alone—as well as our love languages and a dozen other personality quirks, are very different from each other. Especially in the first years of our marriage, these disparities made me feel distant from him. Sometimes I remembered those personality graphs and thought we might be mismatched after all.

When we'd been married for nearly eleven years—right on time if you subscribe to "the eleven-year itch" theory of marital dissatisfaction—we found ourselves in a grim time. I remember looking at him, observing him coolly the way you might look at someone on a subway who is cracking his gum too loudly. I felt nothing except a sort of vague annoyance. The fact that we had young children and a baby on the way, however, made me resolute: we had to work this out. I insisted that we begin marital counseling. If at all possible, my children would not experience the confusion and pain of their parents' divorce. I knew how these had cast long shadows over my own life, and I wanted better for them.

In a time when our identities were shifting and often obscured by the sticky and grueling realities of parenting young children, therapy reminded us of who we were, how our childhood wounds still drove us in our shakiest moments, and, thankfully, how much we loved each other. Therapy was hard work—vulnerable and tear filled. We went weekly for several months, and I count it as one of the wisest decisions we've ever made.

I don't remember everything our therapist said all those years ago, but his words at one of our sessions have stayed with me. "We all think our marriages will heal our childhood injuries," he said, leaning forward in his chair. "But in every marriage, husbands and wives must learn that instead of healing us, issues with our spouses actually open up our old wounds. The couples who last are the ones who work through that pain to a new place, a place of gratitude for what they really have together." In some ways, our therapist said, this is where a real marriage begins.

That bad time did pass, as have others.

Like all our long-married friends, David and I have our own habitual irritations (*Do you have to eat so fast?*), predictable—if insoluble—outbursts (*You don't have any idea how much I'm doing around here!*), and shriller moments of hurt and anger (*Are you even listening to me?*).

John Calvin wrote that God keeps couples from becoming too "complacent or delighted in married life" or too reliant on "mortal blessings" by letting them experience "the shortcomings of their partners" or humbling them with "willful offspring."[2] Put another way, it is good to remember that nothing is certain in life and not to hold too tightly to our blessings—marital or otherwise.

So we've had real struggles—and minor hiccups. Despite David's early strong showing as regards *Harold and Maude*, no matter how hard I've tried for the last three decades, I haven't been able to convince him of the merits of old movie musicals, thick-cut marmalade, or the simple pleasure of sleeping in late. Likewise, he's never won me over to war movies, oysters, or Renaissance music. We still have occasional "divorcial moments," as we call them, when we don't see eye to eye. A brief entry in my journal from a few years ago reads, "Long-Married Couple Files for Divorce after Impassioned Argument about the Merits of the Film *Nebraska*." Movie reviews and marmalade aside, there are times when I mistake his silence for judgment and when I wish he were more talkative, or when we are faced with a parenting dilemma that tangles us up emotionally.

But after all these years, our deepest preferences, convictions, and values dovetail. We share an aversion to fast food, reality television, and bigotry (maybe especially when it's couched in morality talk). We parent our children together well. We love the Episcopal Church. We both wish we lived in a gentler world. And of course, our marriage runs far deeper than that. David sees me as my real—not just projected—self: from the weak and insecure mess of a person whose ego, after reading our friend Jenny's bio years ago, shattered into a million pieces, to the times when I'm at my very best. In our premarital counseling—prior to the personality test debacle— David and I were told that sex is the "oil that keeps the lamp of marriage burning." Ours is a lamp that we maintain; I want us to shine brightly for years to come. And, most of all, we are intentional about being kind. Small acts of courtesy and kindness—bringing the other person a cup of coffee or a glass of water, saying thank you, surreptitiously doing some chore the other one dreads—these have become intrinsic to the way we go through life together.

In short, we are *in*.

A friend posts a status update, tagging his wife, on Facebook:

A wedding anniversary is the celebration of love, trust, partnership, tolerance, and tenacity. The order varies in any given year. Thanks for 20 YEARS of all the above, my dearest!

I think long-married people are less likely than newlyweds to use phrases like *soul mate* or *better half* to describe each other, and more likely—like that Facebook friend—to use a word like *partner*. I wouldn't say David is my best—or perhaps it's more accurate to say "only best"—friend. Although he is my most present, loyal, and deepest friend, I have a several "best" friends, and each one fulfills a different role in my life. There are "best friends" who are my parenting confidants and others with whom I can simply relax and chat for hours. Other friends challenge me intellectually or spiritually. There are some with whom I share long histories. But there's no one like David in my life, no one with whom I've ever shared so intimately than him—not only physically, but also emotionally and in terms of the life we've built together. I trust him fully. But are we "soul mates"? Honestly, I'm not even sure what that term means. I know we're different. He still zigs when I zag. But we have, over the decades, been faithful, fallen in love (and out of love, to be clear) with each other many times, and built our life and family together.

It's also a funny paradox that, as we have grown closer in midlife, David and I have individuated in new ways. We take more trips on our own or with other friends. There's an ease with which we decide when to spend time together as a couple, as a family, or with our own friends. And I can't think of a time when I've felt closer to him or more aware of us as a "we."

David turned fifty last year, and I threw him a surprise party. I had a vision for the evening: one long table (made up of a few smaller ones) set for twenty some people down the center of our dining and living rooms, votive candles, handmade birth-day banners, and tapas from his favorite Spanish restaurant. The day of the party, I sent David out with our youngest, Mia, for an outing in the city. My eldest took the train home from college. A friend came from San Diego, and David's brother flew in from Boston. One of his grad school buddies, our priest, and several other dear friends were there. I didn't invite *my* best friends and their husbands—I invited just the people whom I know that David has long considered his oldest, closest friends. Mia had successfully swept David away for their outing, and the rest of us set up a makeshift photo booth, organized the tables, and prepared for the party.

That night, as we sat at that long table, the candles flicker-ing, almost every one of David's closest friends—from boyhood through graduate school and to the present—took turns stand-ing and sharing favorite memories about him. As they spoke, one after the other, I realized that my husband and I had left our individual selves behind somewhere along the way in our mar-riage. He and I, truly, were a "we." I already knew, of course, that we were "we" to our children. We are "Mom and Dad" or, with a sigh, "the 'rents." But to all these old friends, we were "Jen and David," "David and Jen." I felt humbled to be included in this little phrasing—to hear how "David and Jen were there for me" or "Jenni and David said . . ." I'd never, before the night of his fiftieth, seen myself through the eyes of his friends. I wasn't just David's wife; I had become an inextricable part of the person they knew and loved so well. I guess this is what almost thirty years of marriage will do.

"If we commit ourselves to one person for life this is not, as many people think, a rejection of freedom," Madeleine L'Engle writes. Rather, "it demands the courage to move into all the risks of freedom, and the risk of love which is permanent; into that love which is not possession, but participation. To marry is the biggest risk in human relations that a person can take."[3]

I agree. When we "forsake all others," we limit ourselves on purpose. We begin a kind of vocation and give ourselves the chance to go deep and to die to the self in new—and often difficult—ways. And marriage is hard—but not because of silly things like arguing over which way the toilet paper should hang or whether someone prefers *Full Metal Jacket* to *Singin' in the Rain*. Marriage is very hard because growing up is very hard.

Author and pastor Nadia Bolz-Weber famously welcomes new members to her church by guaranteeing, from day one, that she *will* let them down. "We will disappoint you," she says. "It's a matter of *when*, not if." Bolz-Weber promises that she'll "say something stupid" and hurt their feelings, but says that if they "choose to leave when we don't meet their expectations, they won't get to see how the grace of God can come in and fill the holes left by our community's failure, and that's just too beautiful and too real to miss."[4]

When I first read that, I thought: Isn't that *exactly* like marriage? We all say stupid things, hurt each other's feelings, and let each other down. But . . . it's too beautiful and real to miss.

Last January, one of our nieces got married. It was a happy day—it seemed indisputable that the couple was perfectly matched. (No unsettling personality tests for them!) At the reception, my husband, kids, and I were seated at a small table, set just for the six of us. Instead of the usual dreaded fate at wedding dinners—when we're assigned to tables with strangers and we anxiously labor to make small talk all night, my family and I spent the evening tucked away in the corner of the room, talking and laughing and feeling all of a kind. It is the only wedding reception in my memory—including my own—when I wished I could stay longer. Before leaving the table for the dance floor, we were asked to fill out a card with our best advice to the newly married couple. I knew just what I wanted to say. We passed the pens around the table and scrawled our names and answers. As we left to go dance, I pushed my chair in and flipped over the card at David's place to peek at what he had written. When I saw his card, I had to smile. We had written exactly the same words.

"Always be kind."

SEVENTEEN

Five Simple Lessons Learned in a Botanical Garden

The gardener was a hippie; there was no mistaking it. Sixtysomething, her long gray hair hung in two loose braids, framing a sun-weathered face. When she gestured toward anything from a cactus to a fruit tree, she would ask, slack-jawed and with wide, wondering eyes, "Isn't that *way cool?*" I didn't ask her about Woodstock or whether she'd read *Hitchhiker's Guide to the Galaxy* or how good she was at playing Hacky Sack. I didn't need to.

My husband and I were by far the youngest on the walking tour of the botanical gardens. Our children had opted out: two were watching European football in the condo and the other two seemed truly offended that we'd suggest they squander ninety minutes of their Florida vacation learning about plants. ("*Plants!*")

"And, anyway, it's so *hot*," one of my daughters protested. So David and I were on our own with the hippie gardener and four other couples, seniors and retirees from the Sunshine State, from Puerto Rico, and from Arizona.

Happily, I didn't let the raging sun or my children's antipathy toward the outing keep me indoors, because in addition to seeing stunning flowers and trees, the gardener's words echoed with spiritual wisdom, much needed and lush reminders after a long Chicago winter of the soul.

1. SOMETIMES IT TAKES A VERY LONG TIME TO BLOOM

One of our first stops on the tour was in front of an enormous agave plant; about five feet tall and with long, pointed, spiky leaves. It grew in view of the ocean, in the grass just beyond the sand.

"You'll have to come back and join me here in forty-five years," the gardener said. "She only blooms once in a hundred years, but when she does it's *way cool*."

I looked around at the other people in our group. Some of us likely wouldn't be alive in five years, let alone forty-five. When that agave next blooms, I'll be in my nineties, if I live that long. I pictured returning here with David, so long from now. We'd be gray-haired, longtime empty nesters, great-grandparents. Maybe we'd need to use walkers or wheelchairs, but someone could help us down to the beach to see the agave.

I had a momentary pang of disappointment; it would be so long before this plant bloomed.

But another thought soon followed. It was a comfort to know that life goes on after we die, that in forty-five years and then in another hundred years, this plant (should the hurricanes be kind and the gardeners attentive) will come to flower.

And there was no rushing this late and infrequent bloomer. Its moment would come again, and it would be stunning.

2. PRUNING IS THE KEY TO WITHSTANDING HARSH STORMS

Looking up into the branches of a vibrant red frangipani, an elderly gentleman from Arizona asked how these trees withstand the whipping, hurricane-strength winds.

"Look up high. See how clean the branches are?" the gardener asked. "We keep these trees well pruned so that when strong winds come, they can move through, and we don't give them anything to hang on to."

Roots that go deep and clean branches, she explained, keep trees standing firm in storms.

3. IT TAKES TIME TO HEAL

The gardener showed us how an invasive plant had attached itself to a magnolia tree, twisting and strangling its limbs. The tree was obviously in distress. Unlike its neighbors, it seemed naked, held in a punishing chokehold.

"I've been working on that one for a while," the gardener said with a sigh. "The trick for us is to get rid of the attacker without hurting the host. It takes time to win some battles against these toxic attackers so that the tree can heal and then grow again."

4. WE CAN'T DO EVERYTHING AT ONCE

As we wound around sidewalks and garden paths, our guide told us about each of her predecessors and their areas of expertise.

The first gardener, she said, was a globe-trotting tropical plants expert. It is thanks to him that the gardens were rich with exotic plants and trees. Another loved fruit trees, as evidenced by the key lime, lemon, banana, orange, mango, avocado, and star fruit trees that hung with fruit. Our current gardener loved plants native to that part of Florida.

"Each of us has had a passion for the garden, but each has been different from the last," she explained. "And, over time, the gardens grow in complexity. But we can't do everything all at once."

5. THE GOOD FRUIT IS READY AND WAITING FOR US

Near the end of our tour, we were startled to see a figure crouching behind a stand of bamboo beside a wall.

"Hey there, friend," the gardener called. "Can I help you with something?"

A guest staying at a neighboring resort crawled out of the brush with dead palm fronds and other natural detritus clinging to her dress. She appeared to be in her late eighties, a plucky little woman who admitted that she'd been looking for mangoes.

"The mangoes are good to eat," the gardener said. "But don't get them off the ground back there. Anything left on the ground is rotten or has been nibbled on by a critter. My staff walks the property every day and picks all the fruit from the trees that is ready to eat. It's in a basket in the office. Go on in and help yourself."

The woman pulled a misshapen mango from a pocket in her dress and let it drop into the grass.

At the conclusion of the tour, my husband and I thanked our guide and walked into the cool of the office. We found the mangoes and took a few home to share with the children. Later that afternoon, we peeled and ate them, the thick, sweet juice dripping over our hands and chins.

EIGHTEEN

The U-Curve of Happiness

I get a text from a friend who's spent the past week in and out of doctors' offices and medical labs. Perimenopause has reared its peevish head and flung her into ultrasounds and mammograms and blood tests; she's forty-four. "Have I mentioned how much I'm not enjoying my forties?" she writes. "I'm sitting in the lobby of the clinic. In a bit of a daze. Trying to breathe."

Another friend, also a couple of years younger than me, writes, detailing her struggle with "a new kind" of depression. She says she lacks motivation and that she feels like "a puppet on a string." In her forties, she says, she's felt emotionally flat—except at those times when hormonal swings turn her feelings upside down and spin her into a storm. Her kids are in middle school—that time in a mother's life when she will, as the researchers say, fare most poorly as a parent. I remember feeling topsy-turvy just like she is, a few years ago, and I say her name in prayer.

A Facebook friend, someone I know to be a generally upbeat soul, posts a status update on the eve of her fiftieth birthday: "Farewell to you, oh decade of my 40s!" she writes. "Farewell, you awful wench!"

I believe things are about to improve for these three forty-something friends, and I tell them this whenever I can.

In an article on midlife, writer Jonathan Rauch tells the story of hearing, a decade before he'd need to know it, that "midlife crisis begins sometime in your 40s, when you look at your life and think, *Is this all*? And it ends about 10 years later, when you look at your life again and think, *Actually, this is pretty good*."[1]

Rauch—as have the dozen or so people with whom I've spoken about this phenomenon—says that it was in his fifties when "the fog of disappointment and self-censure began to lift." His article describes the concept of "the U-curve" of happiness. Also known as the U-bend, the theory describes how our sense of well-being and contentment falls from the time we are in our early twenties until we "hit bottom"—and enter what some call a "midlife crisis"—in our forties. (The average age, globally, that people hit this lowest point is forty-six.) But then, despite declining physical attractiveness, poorer eyesight and hearing, and other indignities—and despite losses such as our kids leaving home, the death of people we love, and so on—something surprising happens. We become, progressively, *happier*. We move through that rocky transition into midlife and find something better on the other side. "Something," Rauch writes, "like wisdom."

My friend Mandy agrees. She's fifty-three and says she loves her life now but quickly warns me that she "won't even talk about" her thirties and forties. Maybe we get happier beginning in our late forties because we know ourselves better than we did before. Maybe we've gotten used to who we are. For many women—and men—who have given much of their attention for the last few decades to raising children, moving out of the child-rearing years leaves us with more energy and mental space. We get more sleep. We have more time for ourselves. We're not frantically trying to "balance" our work and home lives. Often, in midlife, women enter a time of renewal and come into our own—in relationship with our bodies, our ambitions, and our gifts—in a new way. All that energy that we parents have been investing in raising children yearns to be put to use elsewhere. We trade in our minivans for smaller cars, glance up from wiping down the countertops, and take a good, hard look at the world and our place in it. Now that our children no longer need us the way they used to, maybe someone or something else does.

I've found it's also in this new stage when, given more time and focus, I can reinvest in relationships that have lain fallow for years. I've been delighted to pick up with old friends who have also been keeping their heads down while raising kids and building their careers. Friends I've not had the resources—time, money, energy—to see regularly or connect with in a deeper way for ten, twenty, even thirty years. But the history and affection we once shared haven't diminished over time. These friendships were just stored away, like twinkly Christmas lights in the attic, unplugged and patiently waiting for December, while we were hard at work in other parts of our lives. Reuniting with such friends—in places as far-flung as Edinburgh, Scotland, or Falls Church, Virginia, or Grand Rapids, Michigan—is a gift of midlife. I'm reminded of who I was before my life became so fully defined as a parent . . . and, I realize, it's still who I am. That true self, underneath the scaffolding.

My friend Mandy says, "Just over the past year or two, I've felt more like myself after years and years of thinking I'd lost my way. I feel more aggressive, more ambitious than I have since I was in my twenties. I feel like I know myself again."

She says she thinks it has something to do with being post-menopausal. I imagine she's right. Its opening notes are hard to hear, but the dramatic opera that women's bodies perform in perimenopause lasts somewhere between two and ten years (the average is four). And then, when the curtain closes, no one misses its hot flashes, night sweats, insomnia, or uneven moods. I've learned that most women *do* feel a new sense of empower-ment after menopause—despite irksome chin hairs and deeper smile lines. Now, nearly on the other side of it, I feel more like myself. Several months ago, I mentioned this to David. "Yeah," he said. "I've noticed. Nothing much rattles you anymore. You seem calmer. More at home in your body."

Of course, we're all different. Last year, after hearing that I was writing a book about midlife, a woman approached me at a Christmas party. She said it would be a crime if I wrote about midlife and didn't talk about how differently both women and men experience our bodies….how, after about age forty or fifty, we're less at home in them and that sex is "no longer a part of the picture."

"Your body changes, and you don't want sex anymore. And your partner doesn't care. He doesn't want it either," she said. "You just completely lose interest in him. You have to write about that in your book."

Although I've heard stories like hers, I've also heard from people who say just the opposite. Some women, knowing they are no longer at risk of becoming pregnant, feel freer in terms of sexual expression. Getting a full night's sleep helps too. (It's hard to feel frisky when you've been up every hour on the hour with a colicky baby, or when your nights are interrupted by requests for glasses of water, or when teenagers are sneaking in way past curfew, or when you are plagued by pesky doubts about what in the world you're doing with your life.) As these distractions dissipate, we might be more interested in sex. And, for some women, the hormonal changes that attend menopause leave them with an increased libido.[2] Of course, generalizations aren't very helpful, and none of this is one size fits all. Except, maybe, the U-curve of happiness.

A friend's Facebook status update, on a later-forty birthday:

Thanks, friends, for all the love.

I wish I had known, when I was younger, that things would turn out fine.

On midlife, theologian Karl Barth wrote: "The sowing is be-hind; now is the time to reap. The run has been taken; now is the time to leap. Preparation has been made; now is the time for the venture of the work itself."[3] Our increased happiness after transitioning into midlife—this tendency to leap—likely has to do with satisfaction in our work, too. We feel less stress because we've either already achieved our professional goals or we have a more realistic view of our gifts and talents. Or we have learned to integrate our jobs with other parts of our lives. I see this play out in the lives of so many forty- and fiftysomething friends, and I see it in my husband's life. In our first decade of marriage, David worked in the theater as an actor. To help pay the rent, he took "day jobs"—tutoring, office work, and so on. But then, not long before our first child was born, he made an abrupt career change and began working in software. We'd joke that he needed to keep his identity as a stage actor "in the closet" so that the engineers would take him seriously. And, for the most part, he did.

In his forties, however, David had to face up to the fact that he sorely missed acting, and he began taking roles in regional theater productions. And then, five years ago after he was cast in a show, he posted flyers at work, at our church, and around the neighborhood about his upcoming performance. Many co-workers and neighbors, people who had only known him as a software developer, the girls' softball coach, or one of the dads on the elementary school playground, came to the show. And instead of taking him less seriously at work, his colleagues have begun asking him to give presentations and use his gifts as a communicator in new ways. I remember seeing a change come across him the year he integrated who he is as an actor with the rest of his life. He was, in a word, happier.

When our kids were young, David and I would watch—with envy and with wonder—as married couples, people older than we were, walk companionably past our house toward the park. They weren't pushing strollers or burdened by diaper bags or dragging a wagon behind them. They just . . . walked. I remember David saying, "Someday that will be us. We'll be able to go on walks like that. Just the two of us." That day has come. We go on long bike rides together. Just the two of us. We can even take weekend trips away together, leaving the kids alone—under the watchful eyes of our neighbors—with the keys to the van and a credit card to order pizza. (So far, so good.) It's as though all that hard work—the teaching and the time-outs, the relationships we've built with our kids, and yes, even keeping commitments like going to soccer games on Saturday mornings—has finally begun to bloom. We can trust them, and we can let them go. Letting go of the way things were, embracing what is.

Several months ago, with a half hour to spare before I needed to pick up one of my daughters at school, I stopped in at a resale shop. It was a tiny place, the walls hung with old wooden signs, the shelves stacked with Nancy Drew books and vases made of pewter or rose glass, and knickknacks. I circled through the shop quickly, but before I stepped out, a snippet of conversation caught my attention and pulled me back in. The owner of the shop was talking with a coworker who'd just come through the back door.

"Oh hey! Glad you're here. I didn't want to tell you the whole thing over the phone," the shop owner said. "So, like I was saying, we got to talking and she said her dad left the family when she was little. And so she grew up without a father—just like me! She's had to deal with some of the fallout from that, I mean, emotionally, since then. You know . . . we've gone around and around about this . . ."

"Yep, we sure have," the friend said.

I found myself standing in the corner of the shop, glued to the story, a story that started, at least, the way I might begin my own. I picked up a tarnished pewter pitcher, pretended to examine it, and set it down, just in case there was a security camera and the women were watching me.

"So he lived out of state and she never saw him after she was like nine or ten—just like me!" the woman continued. (*And me!* I thought.) "And she was always wishing for a father. Jealous when her friends had these great dads, wondering what that would be like. She said she always wanted to be someone's 'princess' or go to father-daughter dances or have a dad to interview boys before they were allowed to take her out."

"You're kidding me," I heard the friend say. "You've always said stuff like that."

"I know!"

The floor creaked where I was standing; I moved a few feet farther into the store and ran my finger along the top of an iron candleholder.

Over the years, I've felt beaten over the head with stories about the lingering insecurity faced by children whose parents have divorced. At least one author calls it "ontological insecurity."[4] The idea is that security and safety are fundamental to our existence, so when parents divorce, there is a lasting rift in the sense of well-being of the child, one that will never heal. That kind of message had woven a net around me that I'd felt tangled in ever since I was a little girl. I didn't want to hear, one more time, how permanently damaged, ill, or broken people were destined to be after their parents divorced—even though, I'll admit, I'd had some of the same thoughts as this store owner as I wondered what it might be like to grow up with a father at home.

I moved around a corner and pulled an antique book of poems from one of the shelves.

"So finally she found him! She did some big Internet search and figured out where he lived and—get this—road-tripped with her boyfriend to see him!"

"No way."

"Yeah. She didn't tell him she was coming or anything, but you know what?"

"Tell me!"

"He didn't even recognize her. She rang the bell and stood there. He was the one who answered . . . but from the second the door opened, she knew. She just *knew*."

"Knew what?"

"That she was *so much* better off with the life that she already had. The life she always had," the storeowner said. "She was better off all along. Better off without him all her life. His apartment was super dirty and depressing and everyone in there—his new family, I guess—looked completely miserable. She realized that it wasn't like she had missed daddy-daughter dances and all that stuff. She had actually been *spared*."

"OMG!" her friend said. "And so . . ."

"And so she said she had the wrong place, and she turned around, and just left! She and her boyfriend got back in the car and drove all the way home. It was like eight hundred miles or something and they drove straight through. And when she told me, I realized it is the same for me!" the storeowner said. "After all these years feeling bad about growing up with just my mom, I get it. *That* was the gift. I was spared. I mean, it seems so obvious. I can't believe I never saw it before. It was a gift all along."

I steadied myself on a ceramic urn. Her story, their story, this story was mine. I'd spent so much time earlier in life dreaming about an ideal that was never realized, but all along I'd been spared from a harsher reality. What I *had* was the gift.

"Oh hey," the shop owner called to me. "Can I help you with anything?"

"No, thanks," I called weakly. "I'm just, you know . . ."

"Sure, look around and let me know if I can help you out," she called.

Oh, sister. You have. You already have, I thought. I walked out of the store feeling as if that net had been untangled and pulled off my heart. I was freed from one more vestige of my childhood perceptions, from the remnants of so much angst over what *wasn't*, and now I saw what *was* in a new way, with clear eyes. The good, the grace, had been around me all the time, like those vases and knickknacks and books on these shelves, and I finally had the eyes to see it.

NINETEEN

The Bridesmaids and the Oil

My friend Tripp is a much more dedicated Facebook user than I am, with multiple posts a day—check-ins and live-stream videos and public posts addressed to "The Internets" or "Facebookistan." ("Y'all be good," he'll say, signing off for the night. "Be excellent to each other, Facebookistan.") An ecumenicist, liturgiologist, and self-proclaimed dillydallier, Tripp came to fatherhood later in life. He and his wife have a very young—and much loved—son, whom they raise together as Tripp completes his doctorate in liturgy and ethnomusicology in Berkeley, California.[1]

When Ernest Hemingway won the Nobel Prize in Literature in 1954, he said, "Writing, at its best, is a lonely life."[2] I've also found the writing life stunningly lonely at times, but interacting online with friends, including Tripp, makes it less so. Meeting Tripp at the virtual water cooler (also known as Facebook) and reading his thoughts on everything from the purposes of boredom to the intersection of music and theology to what it's like to enter fatherhood in his forties are good breaks from hearing only the sound of my own voice.

A recent update:

> Why is it that so very often the great hero or heroine on a quest is still a youth and not some middle aged person? #AskingForAFriend #StartingOverInMy40s.

Responses from Facebookistan, by the way, came quickly, and they heavily relied on *The Lord of the Rings*. One friend said, "Channel your inner Gandalf," and another, "Frodo was 50 when he set out on his quest—and Aragorn was 87!" (How I love Tolkien geeks.)

On Sunday mornings, Tripp "checks in" to his church on Facebook. When I get the notifications, Sunday after Sunday after Sunday, that he's at All Souls Episcopal Parish in Berkeley, I feel a sense of connection not only with other Episcopalians but also with all people of faith who carve out time to worship and pray, separating themselves from their work and all the other usual noise and pleasures that fill up their lives.

Jesus said that we are to receive the kingdom of heaven "like little children" (see Matthew 18:3; Matthew 19:14; Mark 10:13-16; Luke 18:15-17), and attending a church service seems like one example of childlike faith to me. We relinquish our egos for an hour or two, suspend our disbelief, and give ourselves over to the service. We're present in worship in ways we often aren't in the rest of our lives. We wrest our attention away from our glowing phone screens, leaving them turned off, or even—gasp—at home for the morning. We face the same direction, kneel together, and, taking turns, receive the Eucharist. We accept the people around us, just because they happen to be there, much as children who have never before met will share the slide or monkey bars at the playground. In healthy places of worship, we set aside—with varying degrees of success, of course—divisions, doubts, insecurities, and other obstacles to our faith. We know there is so much we don't know or understand, but still we participate. We're all in. We come, in a way, like children.

A few years ago, I was in the Bay Area, and I knew I needed to visit Tripp's church, this place whose name flashes on the screen of my phone every Sunday. On a warm fall morning, I slipped into a pew near the back of All Souls, just in front of a man wearing a neon green T-shirt bearing the image of a cannabis leaf. It read "Keep Calm and Smoke Weed." It was, after all, Berkeley.

The priest who gave the homily that day, the Reverend Liz Tichenor, preached on the parable of the ten bridesmaids (Matthew 25:1-13).[3] It was one of those sermons that seemed to be precisely what I, as a person edging out of my forties, needed to hear. I sat transfixed, forgetting that I was far from home, forgetting the incongruent message and blinding green of the T-shirt worn by the guy behind me, and even forgetting about the long-awaited trip to San Francisco that would begin just after the service.

I was initially disappointed to hear Christ's parable of the bridesmaids read that morning, and even more so when I realized that the priest was choosing to preach on it. It's one of those parts of the Bible that my friend Cathleen calls "clobber verses." These are passages that can be used as weapons of judgment and division, messages that seem to prove that some of us are "in" and some of us are "out" of God's favor and kingdom. For ever and ever and *ever*. It seems to be all about the *afterlife* for some people of faith.

A few years ago, a friend who is a committed environ-
mentalist told me that one of the reasons she isn't interested
in Christianity has to do with her very religious Christian
neighbors. She'd noticed that the family opted out of re-
cycling and treated their lawn with toxic chemical sprays.
When they bought a gigantic, gas-guzzling SUV, my friend
said she couldn't help but to ask about it, noting that as a
person of faith, her neighbor might want to consider the
impact—"you know, on 'God's creation'"—of driving this
vehicle around town.

"Oh, I'm just visiting here. Passing through," the neighbor
laughed. "I'm living for the next world. It doesn't matter if we
trash this one."

Of course, many Christians reject that idea. N. T. Wright,
for example, is a conservative New Testament scholar who in
his book *Surprised by Hope* did indeed surprise some of his
readers when he asserted that modern Christians *profoundly*
misunderstand what the Scriptures say about heaven. In an interview for *Time* magazine, Wright said, "Much of 'traditional'
Christianity gives the impression that God has these rather
arbitrary rules about how you have to behave, and if you dis-
obey them you go to hell, rather than to heaven. What the
New Testament really says is God wants you to be a renewed
human being helping him to renew his creation, and his resurrection was the opening bell."[4] The "kingdom of heaven," then,
isn't located somewhere up among the clouds. It's *here*—and
we are privileged to be a part of it by working for justice, renewal, and hope.

In my tradition, we don't obsess over heaven and hell. The
idea that God rewards some with the gift of eternal life in
heaven and damns the wayward with everlasting, fiery torment
is the antithesis to what I hope is true of God, and what I find

in the Bible, again and again. *God is love. The greatest of these is love. God's love is unfailing for all humanity.* (See 1 John 4:8; 1 Corinthians 13:13; Psalm 36:7). When I hear Christians talk with certainty and judgment about the right way to discern who *is* and who *isn't* going to hell, or imply that the kingdom of heaven is synonymous with the afterlife, I back away slowly. I am hopeful that all things and all of humankind and all of creation will ultimately be renewed by, and reconciled to, God. In Acts 3:21, the apostle Paul refers to God's promise to restore all things in the end. I believe we get to be a part of it; that we're compelled to be a part of this restoration. It's a duty *and* a privilege.

Theologian Peter Rollins so beautifully writes, "Faith, then, is not a set of beliefs about the world. It is rather found in the loving embrace of the world."[5]

In church this past Sunday, our gospel reading included the story of Jesus telling the disciples that when they obey him, they shouldn't expect some big show of thanks or attention, but that they should recognize they are simply doing their duty as his followers when they do good work and have faith (Luke 17:10). When I obey Christ and live intentionally—trying to advance the restoration of God's creation—I am, simply put, just doing my job.

A prayer attributed to Saint Teresa of Ávila reads:

Christ has no body but yours,

No hands, no feet on earth but yours,

Yours are the eyes with which he looks compassion on this world,

Yours are the feet with which he walks to do good,

Yours are the hands, with which he blesses all the world.

Trying to digest and apply these words is a prodigious enough life task for me; I'll leave it up to others to puzzle out the intricacies of the afterlife.

Flip through the Sunday bulletin at my church—and many Christian churches—and you'll find plentiful signs that the congregation is doing their duty to make life less like a hell and more like heaven to those in need. In short, our faith prompts us to love others. One hilarious headline from the *Onion* reads: "Local Church Full of Brainwashed Idiots Feeds Town's Poor Every Week." A quote from the fictitious news story:

> "Unfortunately, there are a lot of people in town who have fallen on hard times and are unable to afford to put food on the table, so we try to help out as best we can," said 48-year-old Kerri Bellamy, one of the mindless sheep who adheres to a backward ideology and is incapable of thinking for herself, while spooning out homemade shepherd's pie to a line of poor and homeless individuals.[6]

But, then, what does a person like me do with parables such as the ten bridesmaids that was read that Sunday in Berkeley? In this one, Jesus says the kingdom of heaven will be like ten bridesmaids who take lamps to await a bridegroom at night. Five are wise and bring extra oil for their lamps. Five are foolish and do not; their lamps run out while they are waiting. The foolish ones ask the others to borrow a bit of oil, but the wise ones refuse, telling them to go shopping and "buy some for yourselves" (Matthew 25:9). (This hardly seems fair. Were any shops open at that hour? It's not like ancient Galilee had a 7-Eleven with a shelf of lamp essentials over by the Slurpee machine.)

But off they go and, unfortunately, while they are away, the bridegroom finally arrives. He welcomes the five wise bridesmaids into the wedding feast and bolts the door behind them. When the "foolish" ones return from their shopping trip, he won't let them in. "Believe me, I don't know you!" he shouts (Matthew 25:12).

Ugh. Really, Jesus? *No feast for you!*

This seems like an uncharacteristic message from Christ. Don't his parables generally seem to shout grace, upend expectations, and encourage generosity and forgiveness? But when you do a quick online search on the bridesmaids parable, you find many preachers asserting that the five wise ones represent the "truly saved" and the foolish ones represent "fake Christians" or people who follow other religions or who practice no religion at all. So is it just a clobber passage after all?

Sitting in Tripp's church, I held my breath—how would the priest handle this tricky passage?

"So what gives?" the Reverend Tichenor began.

No second chances? Just be wise and look out for number one? Often, this parable is used to depict the final judgment, a fearful reckoning of who's in and who's out. But based on the totality of the gospels, I simply don't believe that anyone who seeks God will be definitively shut out of the party. That doesn't follow from the rest of what Jesus teaches—the Good Shepherd goes to the ends to find the one lost sheep, the father welcomes that wayward son home by pulling out all the stops, and as Paul writes in our epistle, even the dead are not beyond the reach of Christ's love.[7]

The Rev. Tichenor said that, like the bridesmaids who lacked the oil for their lamps, when we "fail to be present with our whole selves, ready to engage for the long haul, the reality is that we do miss out, and sometimes when we realize it, it's already too late for that particular party."

Sitting in the back of that unfamiliar church, I thought about the losses, the moments of scorching insecurity, and the missed opportunities I'd had over the last decade. Times when I missed a "particular party"—when I wasn't present with my whole self, but instead was blinded by self-consciousness, anxiety, or the sting of envy. Times when my own egotistical navel-gazing blinded me from seeing the gifts all around me. When had I missed opportunities to give my sister oil for her lamp? In what ways had I blinded myself to injustice and the needs of my neighbors? What oil hadn't I shared with my children? My husband? What opportunities had I missed to serve others, in my community and around the world?

I've been both the wise and the foolish bridesmaid, depending on the day. Sometimes I'm focused, prepared, and on task—perhaps to the detriment of those around me. When had I refused to unclench my fists and share, or refused to look around and find a way to engage with those in need? Had I sent people off, shooing them away and directing them to just go elsewhere, when they've needed resources that I have in abundance? The teacher's pet, primly pleased with myself for getting my work finished on time and keeping my desk so clean and organized? Other times I've been nervous and distracted, waylaid and ill-equipped. Lazy and feeling entitled to the oil in other people's lamps, comparing my own life to others, or lost contemplating my identity and sense of worthiness. I've been both types of bridesmaid—switching lamps multiple times during one day.

"And so as we look ahead," the priest said, "let us cast aside our excuses, our fears of not having enough oil or whatever it is we think we need first, and just come, commit, and celebrate. Instead of shrinking away from a door once closed, let's gather our gumption, our resolve, and choose the feast in front of us."

Be engaged. Be prepared. Leave regrets behind. This is an exceptionally good message for me right here in midlife. Now isn't the time to make excuses or ruminate. It's time to move on, with hope. I remembered my desperate, middle-of-the-night prayers asking God to send me a sign or just "meet me halfway." This homily at the church in Berkeley felt like an answer. It was one that was likely there all along, waiting years for me to quiet down and hear it.

Christiane Northrup ends her seminal work *The Wisdom of Menopause* with a similar encouragement: "We're waking up together, you and I. . . . But don't panic if you feel some pain. Whenever we give birth to anything important, like the new relationship with our souls that is possible at midlife, there are going to be labor pains."

A new relationship with my soul. Yes.

"There is enormous power here," Northrup writes. "We're at a turning point. . . . No one yet suspects how much we can accomplish when we go into our businesses, churches, clubs, and families and, quietly and peacefully, like the stealth missiles we are, set about changing everything for the better."[8]

We can begin again, even in midlife, to stand with oil in our lamps, ready to change our communities and world, ready to participate more fully in what some call the "work of the kingdom." And when someone with extraordinary gifts or a great heart dies young—I think of people like Philip Seymour Hoffman, Princess Diana, my sister Susan, my friend Brett Foster, and even my grandparents from Detroit about whom I know so little—we grieve not only for their lives, but also for the contributions they would have made in midlife and beyond—relationally, professionally, spiritually. And, in middle age, we'll be in good company—Mother Teresa tops the greatest hits album of late bloomers. She was forty when she founded

Missionaries of Charity. Or think of Julia Child, Laura Ingalls Wilder, Helen Mirren, Ang Lee—and countless others who were not young when they took full, deep breaths and started off on new quests.

And of course there are millions of other much less celebrated people who came into their own in midlife, changing the world for the better. Saints and students and public servants. They pursue graduate degrees—yes, arrogant sixteen-year-old self, just like those middle-aged students of my mother's in their shoulder pads and acid-washed jeans. They take risks—they start new businesses, adopt children, write books, or quit dependable jobs, finally hearing and answering God's call to live and give with wholehearted intention. They reshape themselves and culture anew in midlife in these ways and countless others. These people—famous or not—reach out to us, extend their hands, and beckon us to wake up and to be engaged. They ask us to come along and bring lamps brimming with oil into this new part of life.

Walking out of that church that Sunday in California, I felt *ready*. At the edge of fifty, I was no longer waiting for my life to start—in terms of my faith or in any other area of life. My prayers had evolved from grabby, ego-driven, four-in-the-morning begging to a deeper acceptance of the mystery of God. I felt a new call to engage for the long haul in the work and life that is mine. Sure, I'd missed out sometimes earlier in life, but there would be many other parties ahead.

EPILOGUE

Like We Were Never Here

I'm sitting in a folding chair next to my husband, our legs stretched out in front of us, our heels resting in the cool grass. We can't see them, but in the pavilion at the other edge of the park, Emmylou Harris and Lyle Lovett sing a haunting duet. A full, white moon rises, finding its place high above the trees, and the other party guests, sitting in the circle of chairs, talk softly or sit back, their eyes closed, soaking up the night.

That evening is drawn into my memory in permanent ink.

There were about twenty of us, friends and family, from all over the country, gathered at an outdoor music venue to surprise my friend Anthony for his fortieth birthday. Coolers and camp chairs and picnic baskets in hand, we ranged in age from twelve to about seventy-five. We were gay and straight. Divorced, married, and single. Various races, backgrounds, political and religious convictions. We shared the evening—food, drink, and conversation—and were strangers brought together because of the common love we have for a friend.

It was as flawless a night as any of us could have hoped for. Anthony was surprised. There was a big Batman cake for our comic book–loving friend, and the moon was decidedly showing off as it stretched its arms wide in the night sky. Anthony's niece did cartwheels in the grass as he introduced each one of us. *This is my support system.* He swept his arms in a broad circle, including us all. We became, for a brief time, community.

But not everything was picture perfect that night—real life always manages to snag us for a second, to seep in, even in those idyllic moments. Standing up front to see the performers, I had to jostle through the crowd for a new spot when a man next to me almost drowned out Lyle, shouting the wrong lyrics to his song. "If I had a pony, I'd go out on the ocean!" he screamed.

Walking back to our patch of grass, I overheard a slightly drinky woman shout, "I'm so boozed that the bum truck is closed." It took me a moment, but then I decided that was the funniest thing I'd heard in about a year. (Telling my son the story later that night, he said, "That's like the old joke: 'Officer, I swear to drunk I'm not God.'") And one in our party, a man with a long-lensed camera, kept taking candid shots of us from a squat beach chair, and I knew the angle (from below and from the side) would result in unflattering pictures. Sure enough, when someone posted all the photos later, I texted Anthony.

"Love the pics from your party. Except that one where I look like Java the Hutt."

"Oh, spare me," he replied. "It's Jabba."

As the concert was ending, Lyle sang "Pass Me Not"— "Savior, hear my humble cry . . . do not pass me by"—a lovely end to the night. We all began packing away the leftover food, corking bottles, folding up blankets. Tables and chairs were collapsed and slid into canvas string bags. Slowly walking toward the parking lot, I fell into step with Anthony's father, Charlie. The moon shone brightly down on the park as though the houselights had been flipped on, the summer night declaring that it was time to go home.

Charlie turned and pointed back at the area we had occupied all evening. "Look at that," he said, his voice bemused. "There's not a trace of us left. It's like we were never here."

We stopped and looked at the spot together.

"And tomorrow night, it will be filled with other people," I said. "And all their chairs and blankets and food and chitchat. It might even be someone else's birthday party."

Delighted, he let out a big laugh. "Oh yes! You're right!" And then we walked on.

A time for everything, I thought. Solomon, the teacher, tells us: "What is happening now has happened before, and what will happen in the future has happened before, because God makes the same things happen over and over again" (Ecclesiastes 3:15).

There is nothing new under the sun. We arrive, we gather, we fill up space and set up camp. We make messes in our "wild and precious lives," as poet Mary Oliver says,[1] and we clean them up. We eat and drink. We share stories, and memories take shape in those strange seahorses in our brains. The moon rises and it sets. We sing out loud together, and sometimes we're off pitch or get the lyrics wrong.

And then the concert ends. We disappear as quickly as we arrived, leaving the space open for the next group of people. They'll share a meal, listen to the music, and create a short-lived community while they're here. None of us can make it last any longer than it will. What we can do, as Solomon writes, is eat and drink and enjoy the fruits of our labor, knowing them to be gifts from God.

And that's just as it always has been, and as it will be.

Acknowledgments

I owe huge thanks to my smart and clever writing communities, including members of INK: A Creative Collective. I'm grateful to Lesa Engelthaler, Rachel Klooster, and Anthony Platipodis who read early drafts of this book; thank you for your prompts, reassurance, and questions—and Anthony, particularly, for your laughter and the bold slashes of your (figurative) red pen. Some of this book was written on writing retreats in Topanga, California; Madison, Connecticut; and West Dulwich, London. I am grateful to the Speranza Foundation's Lincoln City Fellowship for a grant that covered my travel expenses and afforded me solitary time to think. These retreats have been vital to me as a writer.

Thank you to Sandy Koropp at Prairie Path Books in Wheaton, Illinois, for the way you resolutely support readers and writers—and also for riffing about "cheetah readers" when we were brainstorming title ideas and cover design. My thanks to Valerie Weaver-Zercher and Amy Gingerich at Herald Press;

I love working with you. Thanks to my agent, Christopher Ferebee, for abiding support and wisdom.

I'm fortunate to have friendships that have spanned decades—and newer ones that are characterized by such love and understanding that it feels like we've been friends all our lives. Thank you especially to Rose Allison and Sheila Yarrow, Mindy and Carl Alston, Beth Andersen, Amy Julia Becker, Tricia and Michael Benich, Dale Hanson Bourke, Maura and Paul Constance, Ellen Painter Dollar, Becky and Jim Dorf, Suzanne Ecklund, Cathleen Falsani and Maury Possley, Keiko and Rob Feldman, Anise Foster, Grace and Michael Freedman, Sara Hendren and Brian Funck, Bradford Johnson, Andrea and Michael Le Roy, Mary and Mark Lewis, Suzanne Luchs, Katy and Andy Mangin, Rachel Mariner, Anthony Platipodis, Caryn Rivadeneira, James Saba, Jenny and Eric Sheffer Stevens, Susan and Scott Shorney, Thad Smith and Andrea McNaughton, Margot Starbuck, Rachel Marie Stone, Jon Sweeney, Kathy and Jeremy Treat, Sarah Vanderveen, and Cara Whiting. I am thankful, too, to my Haiti delegation friends whom I met through Hope Through Healing Hands. You are world-changers (and, truly, so very much fun). One of the gifts of writing this book was reflecting on how all of you have added joy and meaning to my life.

Mostly, and as ever, I am grateful for my family—David, Theo, Ian, Isabel, and Mia.

Notes

Introduction   Memory, Seahorses, and Telling It Slant

1 C. S. Lewis, *A Grief Observed* (New York: Faber and Faber, 1961), 54.

2 Emily Dickinson, "Tell All the Truth but Tell It Slant" (1129), in *The Complete Poems of Emily Dickinson* (Boston: Back Bay Books, 1976), 506.

3 Gabriel García Márquez, *Love in the Time of Cholera* (New York: Penguin Books, 1989), 106.

4 Carol Tavris and Elliot Aronson, *Mistakes Were Made (but Not by Me): Why We Justify Foolish Beliefs, Bad Decisions, and Hurtful Acts*, rev. ed. (New York: Mariner Books, 2015), 97–98.

5 Richard Rohr, *Falling Upward: A Spirituality for the Two Halves of Life* (London: SPCK Publishing, 2012).

6 Mary Karr, *The Art of Memoir* (New York: HarperCollins, 2015), 153.

Chapter 1   Yahweh, Meet Me Halfway

1 Read more about the Heidelberg Project at www.heidelberg.org.

2 See Suniya S. Luthar and Lucia Ciciolla, "What It Feels Like to Be a Mother: Variations by Children's Developmental Stages," *Developmental Psychology* 52, no. 1 (January 2016): 143–54.

3 Stephanie DeGraff Bender, *The Power of Menopause: A Woman's Guide to Physical and Emotional Health during the Transitional Decade* (New York: Three Rivers Press, 1998), 5.

Chapter 2   Jenny's (Better) Bio

1 Timothy Keller, *The Freedom of Self-Forgetfulness: The Path to True Christian Joy* (Youngstown, OH: 10Publishing, 2012), 14.

2 These words are from Paul Simon's song, "You Can Call Me Al," *Graceland*, Warner Brothers Records, 1986. (Honestly, if this song isn't an anthem for midlife, I don't know what is.)

3 This and the quotations in the preceding paragraph are from Marcia Reynolds, "What a Female Mid-Life Crisis Looks Like," *Psychology Today*, May 14, 2011, https://www.psychologytoday.com/blog/wander-woman/201105/what-female-mid-life-crisis-looks.

4 Elinor Lipman, *I Can't Complain: (All Too) Personal Essays* (New York: Mariner Books, 2014), 57.

5 Keller, *The Freedom of Self-Forgetfulness*, 32. The quotation in the previous paragraph, "the court is adjourned," appears on page 44 of Keller's book.

Chapter 3   Middle-Aged Is Actually a Thing

1 J. R. R. Tolkien, *The Fellowship of the Ring: Being the First Part of the Lord of the Rings* (New York: Mariner Books, 2012), 193.

2 C. S. Lewis, *Mere Christianity*, rev. ed. (HarperSanFrancisco, 2009), 121–122.

Chapter 4   Shut-Door Panic

1 J. A. Hazeley and J. P. Morris, *The Ladybird Book of The Mid-Life Crisis* (New York: Penguin/Random House, 2015), 6.

2 Christiane Northrup, *The Wisdom of Menopause: Creating Physical and Emotional Health during the Change*, rev. ed. (New York: Random House/Bantam Books, 2006), 77.

3 O. G. Brim, C. D. Ryff, and R. C. Kessler, *How Healthy Are We? A National Study of Well-Being at Midlife* (Chicago: The University of Chicago Press, 2004).

4 This and the quotation in the preceding paragraph are from Kaleem Aftab, "Juliette Binoche: 'You Have to Be More Intelligent.'" The Talks, November 25, 2015, http://the-talks.com/interview/juliette-binoche/.

Chapter 5   Coyotes and Shadow Selves

1 Carl Jung, *Psychology and Religion: West and East*, vol. 11, *Collected Works of C. G. Jung* (Princeton: Princeton University Press, 1975), 76.

2 Rohr, *Falling Upward*, 128.

3 Kay Warren, *Dangerous Surrender: What Happens When You Say Yes to God* (Grand Rapids: Zondervan, 2007), 24.

4 Peter Rollins, "My Confession: I Deny the Resurrection," Peter Rollins website, January 1, 2009, peterrollins.net/my-confession-i-deny-the-resurrection/.

5 "Baptismal Covenant," The Book of Common Prayer (New York: Church Publishing, 1979), 294.

Chapter 6   Jury Duty

1 Ray Bradbury, "A Sound of Thunder," in *R is for Rocket*. (New York: Doubleday, 1952), 18.

2 Kate Bowler, "Death, the Prosperity Gospel and Me," *New York Times*, February 13, 2016, http://www.nytimes.com/2016/02/14/opinion/sunday/death-the-prosperity-gospel-and-me.html.

3 Lewis, *A Grief Observed*, 56.

4 Frederick Buechner, *Telling Secrets: A Memoir*, repr. ed. (New York: HarperOne, 2000), 92.

5 Richard Rohr, *Everything Belongs: The Gift of Contemplative Prayer* (New York: Crossroad Publishing, 1999), 155–56.

Chapter 7   Contributors' Notes

1 Robert Frost, "The Death of the Hired Man," Poets.org, https://www.poets.org/poetsorg/poem/death-hired-man.

2 Wendell Berry, "The Rising," in *The Wheel* (New York: North Point Press, 1982), 14.

Chapter 8   Holding Up a Mirror

1   William Shakespeare, *Romeo and Juliet*, Act III, sc. 5, lines 160, 187–95.

2   Ibid., Act I, sc. 1, line 87.

3   Joseph Campbell and Bill Moyers, *The Power of Myth* (New York: Anchor, 1991), 68.

Chapter 10   Elton John Glasses

1   This and the quotation in the preceding paragraph are from Laura Kastner and Jennifer Wyatt, *Getting to Calm: Cool-Headed Strategies for Parenting Tweens and Teens* (Mercer Island, WA: Parent Map, 2009), 108.

2   Johnny Marr and Steven Patrick Morrissey, "Stop Me If You Think You've Heard This One Before," in *Strangeways, Here We Come*, Rough Trade Records, 1987.

3   Lisa Damour, *Untangled: Guiding Teenage Girls through the Seven Transitions into Adulthood* (New York: Ballantine Books, 2016), 8.

Chapter 11   Two Truths and a Lie: Parents of Teens Edition

1   Michael Gerson, "Saying Goodbye to My Child, the Youngster," *The Washington Post*, August 19, 2013, https://www.washingtonpost. com/opinions/michael-gerson-saying-goodbye-to-my-child-the -youngster/2013/08/19/6337802e-08dd-11e3-8974-f97ab3b3c677 _story.html?utm_term=.3687d8e6efa4.

Chapter 12   Death Flickering Like a Pilot Light

1 Brett Foster, "Five Citations on Our Hope and Predicament." *Letters Journal* 2 (Spring 2014), 18. In "Five Citations," Foster references William Matthews's poem "Defenestrations in Prague" which ends with the words "death flickering in you like a pilot light." Matthews's poem is found his book *After All: Last Poems* (New York: Houghton Mifflin,1998), 37.

2   L. M. Montgomery, *Anne of Green Gables* (Boston: L. C. Page, 1908), 72.

3 Sylvia Plath, *The Unabridged Journals of Sylvia Plath*, ed. Karen V. Kukil (New York: Anchor, 2000), 199.

4 Mother Teresa, *Come Be My Light: The Private Writings of the Saint of Calcutta* (New York: Doubleday Religion, 2007), 187.

5 Pope Francis, "Homily for the Canonization of Mother Teresa," September 4, 2016, transcript, Vatican Radio, http://en.radiovaticana.va/news/2016/09/04/homily_for_the_canonization_of_mother_teresa_full_text/1255727.

6 Among many other places in the Scripture where God is said to have been influenced by someone's prayer or "relented" or "changed his mind" is Exodus 32:14, which says, "So the Lord changed his mind about the terrible disaster he had threatened to bring on his people."

Chapter 13   What Is Left of Her

1 Jon M. Sweeney, "What Do We Do with Mom's Body?" explorefaith.org, 2003, http://www.explorefaith.org/livingspiritually/body_and_soul/death_burial_and_cremation.php.

2 Ibid.

3 David Sedaris, "Now We Are Five," *New Yorker*, October 28, 2013, http://www.newyorker.com/magazine/2013/10/28/now-we-are-five.

Chapter 14   Melanoma Posters

1 Robertson Davies, *What's Bred in the Bone* (New York: Penguin Books, 1986), 73.

2 Lewis, *A Grief Observed*, 3.

Chapter 16   Lucky in Love

1 There is some dispute about whether Teddy Roosevelt said this or whether the phrase was written by a contemporary writer named Dwight Edwards. (Either way, it's a good reminder.)

2 John Calvin, *Golden Booklet of the True Christian Life* (Grand Rapids, MI: Baker Books, 2004), 69.

3 Madeleine L'Engle, *The Irrational Season* (San Francisco: HarperOne, 1984), 47.

4   Nadia Bolz-Weber, *Pastrix* (New York: Jericho Books, 2013), 54.

Chapter 18   The U-Curve of Happiness

1   Jonathan Rauch, "The Real Roots of Midlife Crisis," *Atlantic*, December 2004, http://www.theatlantic.com/magazine /archive/2014/12/the-real-roots-of-midlife-crisis/382235/.

2   J. L. Shifren and S. Hanfling, *Sexuality in Midlife and Beyond: Special Health Report* (Boston: Harvard Health Publications, 2010).

3   Karl Barth, *Church Dogmatics* (Louisville, KY: Westminster John Knox Press, 1994), 614.

4   Andrew Root. *The Children of Divorce: The Loss of Family as the Loss of Being* (Ada, MI: Baker Academic, 2010)

Chapter 19   The Bridesmaids and the Oil

1   Tripp Hudgins edits and writes for his website, sonictheology.org.

2   Ernest Hemingway, "Banquet Speech," December 10, 1954, written text, read by U.S. ambassador John C. Cabot, http://www .nobelprize.org/nobel_prizes/literature/laureates/1954/hemingway -speech.html.

3   Listen to the entirety of the Reverend Liz Tichenor's November 9, 2014, sermon at http://www.allsoulsparish.org/sermons/20141109.

4   Quoted in David Van Biema, "Christians Wrong about Heaven, Says Bishop," *Time*, February 7, 2008, http://content.time.com/time /world/article/0,8599,1710844,00.html.

5   Peter Rollins, *The Divine Magician: The Disappearance of Religion and the Discovery of Faith* (Brentwood, TN: Howard Books, 2015), 96.

6   "Local Church Full of Brainwashed Idiots Feeds Town's Poor Every Week," *Onion*, January 3, 2014, http://www.theonion.com /article/local-church-full-of-brainwashed-idiots-feeds-town-34860.

7   In her sermon, Tichenor refers to Romans 8:38, which reads, "And I am convinced that nothing can ever separate us from God's love. Neither death nor life, neither angels nor demons, neither our fears for today nor our worries about tomorrow—not even the powers of hell can separate us from God's love."

8 This and the quotation in the earlier paragraph are from Northrup, *The Wisdom of Menopause*, 539.

Epilogue   **Like We Were Never Here**

1 Mary Oliver, "The Summer Day," *New and Selected Poems*, vol. 1, repr. ed. (Boston: Beacon Press, 2004), 94.

The Author

Jennifer Grant is a writer, editor, and speaker. A former health and family columnist for the *Chicago Tribune*, she is the author of five previous books, including the adoption memoir *Love You More* and the daybook *Wholehearted Living*. She is a part of Hope Through Healing Hands' Faith-based *Coalition for Healthy Mothers and Children Worldwide*. Grant is a graduate of Wheaton College (BA) and Southern Methodist University (MA). She is a longtime member of St. Mark's Episcopal Church in Glen Ellyn, Illinois, and she lives in the Chicago area with her husband, David, four children, and two rescue dogs. Find her online at jennifergrant .com or on Twitter @jennifercgrant.

A free discussion guide for this book is available at HeraldPress.com/StudyGuides.